D1403913

DEMCO

Cliques

Other titles in the Hot Topics series include:

Cliques

by Toney Allman

LUCENT BOOKS

A part of Gale, Cengage Learning

GALE
CENGAGE Learning™

Detroit • New York • San Francisco • New Haven, Conn • Waterville, Maine • London

LIBRARY OF CONGRESS CATALOGING-IN-PUBLICATION DATA

Allman, Toney.
  Cliques / by Toney Allman.
    p. cm. -- (Hot topics)
  Includes bibliographical references and index.
  ISBN 978-1-4205-0308-1 (hbk.)
  1. Teenagers--Psychology. 2. Cliques (Sociology) 3. Peer pressure. 4. Interpersonal relations in adolescence. 5. Bullying in schools. 6. School environment--Social aspects. I. Title.
  HQ799.2.P44.A44 2010
  303.3'270835--dc22

                      2010019452

YA 303.327 A 4/11 Gale Grp. 33.45

Lucent Books
27500 Drake Rd.
Farmington Hills, MI 48331

ISBN-13: 978-1-4205-0308-1
ISBN-10: 1-4205-0308-1

Printed in the United States of America
1 2 3 4 5 6 7 14 13 12 11 10

Printed by Bang Printing, Brainerd, MN, 1st Ptg., 09/2010

CONTENTS

FOREWORD

Young people today are bombarded with information. Aside from traditional sources such as newspapers, television, and the radio, they are inundated with a nearly continuous stream of data from electronic media. They send and receive e-mails and instant messages, read and write online "blogs," participate in chat rooms and forums, and surf the Web for hours. This trend is likely to continue. As Patricia Senn Breivik, the former dean of university libraries at Wayne State University in Detroit, has stated, "Information overload will only increase in the future. By 2020, for example, the available body of information is expected to double every 73 days! How will these students find the information they need in this coming tidal wave of information?"

Ironically, this overabundance of information can actually impede efforts to understand complex issues. Whether the topic is abortion, the death penalty, gay rights, or obesity, the deluge of fact and opinion that floods the print and electronic media is overwhelming. The news media report the results of polls and studies that contradict one another. Cable news shows, talk radio programs, and newspaper editorials promote narrow viewpoints and omit facts that challenge their own political biases. The World Wide Web is an electronic minefield where legitimate scholars compete with the postings of ordinary citizens who may or may not be well-informed or capable of reasoned argument. At times, strongly worded testimonials and opinion pieces both in print and electronic media are presented as factual accounts.

Conflicting quotes and statistics can confuse even the most diligent researchers. A good example of this is the question of whether or not the death penalty deters crime. For instance, one study found that murders decreased by nearly one-third when the death penalty was reinstated in New York in 1995. Death penalty supporters cite this finding to support their argument that the existence of the death penalty deters criminals from committing murder. However, another study found that states without the death penalty have murder rates below the national average. This study is cited by opponents of capital punishment, who reject the claim that the death penalty deters murder. Students need context and clear, informed discussion if they are to think critically and make informed decisions.

The Hot Topics series is designed to help young people wade through the glut of fact, opinion, and rhetoric so that they can think critically about controversial issues. Only by reading and thinking critically will they be able to formulate a viewpoint that is not simply the parroted views of others. Each volume of the series focuses on one of today's most pressing social issues and provides a balanced overview of the topic. Carefully crafted narrative, fully documented primary and secondary source quotes, informative sidebars, and study questions all provide excellent starting points for research and discussion. Full-color photographs and charts enhance all volumes in the series. With its many useful features, the Hot Topics series is a valuable resource for young people struggling to understand the pressing issues of the modern era.

INTRODUCTION

"LUNCH TRAY MOMENTS"

In the 2004 film *Mean Girls*, actress Lindsay Lohan's character, Cady, is the new girl at North Shore High School. One of her most important early lessons is where each clique sits at lunch. Woe to anyone who sits at the wrong table or with the wrong group of students. Cady is invited to sit with the "Plastics," the most popular, powerful, and exclusive girl clique at the school. Other students rigidly choose their "rightful" tables, and some are not welcome anywhere.

Screenwriter Tina Fey based her movie script about mean girls and their cliques on the book *Queen Bees & Wannabes* by Rosalind Wiseman. The nonfiction book describes the roles girls play in the cliques that rule "girl world" in middle and high schools. Wiseman asked real teens to diagram their school's cafeterias, and she discovered that "their worlds are harsh, judgmental places." People are insiders or outsiders, accepted or rejected, and controlled by the way others stereotype and classify them. Social success or humiliation may rest on something as seemingly small as where people sit at lunch and with whom. Wiseman describes one typical lunchtime situation:

> You have a close group of friends, but for some reason one of your best friends . . . tells you that one of your other friends is spreading rumors about you. . . . Thoughts race through your head. What did you do? Why is she mad at you? . . . All of a sudden, a question drives an icy stake of fear through your heart as you stand

there clutching your orange plastic lunch tray in the cafeteria line: Where are you going to sit at lunch?"[1]

Wiseman calls experiences like this "lunch tray moments"[2] and says they are examples of the extreme social pressures faced by teens in school. Both boys and girls, according to Wiseman, group themselves into cliques. Most people do not like the label "clique." They prefer to say they have a "group." They may insist, "We don't have cliques," or "We just all have our own

Cliques expert and author of Queen Bees and Wannabes *Rosalind Wiseman shows a video concerning teen cliques to parents at the Unilever Tween Confidence event in New York City on March 30, 2010.*

friends." But experts say that many friendship groups are indeed cliques, and the members often engage in behavior that excludes and demeans other people. That is why Wiseman always gets affirmative responses in her school workshops when students are asked anonymously if "exclusive cliques"[3] exist in their school. Cliques exist, and often they can be mean.

CIRCLE OF FRIENDS

In 1995 when Philip Guo was twelve years old, he and his family moved from New York to California. There Philip entered the seventh grade, and he was the "new kid." It was not a pleasant experience for him. He noticed immediately that he did not fit in. His clothes were considered unfashionable by the other students. He was a little chubby and combed his hair in a "dorky" way. He was Asian in a predominantly Caucasian school. He was afraid to even try to make friends. He remembers that cliques had already formed among the seventh graders, and he could tell right away who was popular and who was not. The popular groups of people ignored him, as did most of the other students. Philip felt like a loser throughout his seventh-grade year. By the eighth grade, however, his self-confidence improved; he learned about the fashion trends in California and began to dress more like the other students. He combed his hair more stylishly. He learned to act in a more sociable way. Philip says, "I actually made friends with the mainstream group of dorks."[4] Maybe he was not "cool" or part of the popular groups who were the leaders in the school, but Philip was happy in his own friendship group.

Friendship Groups and Fitting In

Experts, such as psychologists, educators, and sociologists, say that Philip's school and his observations there are typical of schools almost everywhere in the United States. The vast majority of students group themselves into small, tight circles of friends within the school. That is what cliques are—friendship groups or social networks that give people a place to belong. Most of the time, cliques are small groups that average about five or six members, who are held together by common interests, values, or traits, and that are formed around one or more leaders. Whether a specific individual shares the characteristics and interests of the clique determines whether that person is included in or excluded from the clique. Philip, for example, enrolled in accelerated classes, along with changing his clothing style, so he had academic choices and interests in common with the boys who accepted him into their eighth-grade friendship group.

Other people may group themselves into cliques based on their interest in music, band, theater, or sports. Some may choose popularity, love of a particular celebrity, video gaming,

The majority of teens group themselves into small, tight circles of friends within their schools.

social class, good looks, or style of dress as defining characteristics in their clique. Many, as Philip discovered, may see race or ethnic group as an important factor in their choice of friendship groups. From 2003 through 2004, for instance, sociologist Jesse Rude studied the cliques in two middle schools in San Francisco, California. The students he interviewed explained that they did not consciously exclude people of different ethnic groups from their cliques. Nevertheless, the fact that they chose friendships with people similar to them or who lived in the same neighborhoods or who had similar cultures and backgrounds meant that most were grouped by race and ethnic background. In the school yard one day, Rude observed Samoan girls grouped together to play basketball, African American girls jumping rope, Latino students together on the school steps, a group of Asian American girls sitting and talking on benches, and African American boys playing a game of basketball. Each clique separated itself by its common interests and by the comfortableness and feeling of closeness that the group imparted to its individual members.

Who Joins Cliques?

A feeling of belonging is perhaps the most important reason that people become members of cliques. Although cliques are a phenomenon that occurs at any age, psychologist Michael G. Thompson says that some children may begin to form cliques as early as the second grade. He also notes, "They are very much in evidence by fourth grade, and they dominate the lives of sixth, seventh, and eighth graders until they begin, mercifully, to fade in high school."[5] Other experts agree that cliques become less important in people's lives by the eleventh or twelfth grade.

Thompson says it is merciful that cliques fade out during high school because cliques often determine status, power, and popularity. They create a hierarchy in school that makes some people feel like losers or limits their social opportunities and that ranks others as important and as leaders of the school. Sometimes cliques can dominate schools or classes and cause harm both to members and outsiders. This does not necessarily mean that cliques are bad, but it does mean that cliques have both positive and negative effects, especially in middle school, when cliques are so common.

The Benefits of Cliques

Joshua Mandel, a psychologist at New York University's Child Study Center, says that cliques form as children reach adolescence. He says that cliques "provide a social niche and help kids develop a sense of belonging, support, and protection. Cliques boost self-esteem by making kids feel wanted, and they enable the clique member to develop a sense of identity and to regulate social interactions." Mandel explains that all these factors are important because teens are experiencing many changes in their bodies and minds as they outgrow childhood. Teens are learning to separate from their families and become more independent. They are coping with physical development that can make them feel awkward and worried about their looks and normality. They are working to establish social relationships in which they are accepted for themselves. Parents and family often become less important than friends as young people try to learn who they are and what kind of person they want to be. Yet, struggling to understand where one fits in the world can cause a lot of uncertainty and insecurity. Mandel calls adolescence a "tough and exciting time."[6]

During this time, teens are also adjusting to changes at school. In the United States, as children grow older, they progress from elementary schools to middle schools, which are often large and impersonal places. In some of them, students are known more by their ID card numbers than by their names. Students also face increased academic demands, different teachers for different subjects, and judgments about their behavior and worth from other students and teachers. Joining a clique can be a very healthy part of growing up, especially as school and social life become so stressful. Close circles of friends, or cliques, make growing up and feeling safe and secure about all these challenges much easier for cliques members. Sometimes, according to clique expert and writer Rosalind Wiseman, school can feel like a war zone. In her book, *Queen Bees & Wannabes*, Wiseman writes, "I see them [cliques] as platoons of soldiers who have banded together to navigate the perils and insecurities of adolescence."[7]

Children can form cliques as early as second grade.

How Cliques Function

Just like a platoon of soldiers, cliques often are organized with leaders and followers. The leader may be the person who feels the most self-confident and popular. He or she may feel powerful, liked, and important just by being the leader. However, followers in the clique feel liked, accepted, and important, too. Everyone in the clique knows that they have a close circle of friends who provide a safe haven. Their friends will support them, include them in social activities, share secrets and interests, and stand with them in times of trouble. Clique members can have the feeling of "us against the world" as they move through the complex, sometimes frightening and threatening, world of school.

Just like soldiers, clique members may also have "uniforms" that mark them as belonging together. They may adopt a special style of dress or choose certain clothing brands or jewelry

Clique members often adopt special types of dress or jewelry to identify themselves as part of a clique.

that identifies them as part of the clique. Rules about behavior may govern the clique, too. These rules ensure that everyone fits in and that they share the same values and attitudes. Conforming to clique rules can be important because being different or standing out is often stressful for young people who care about fitting in with their peers as they practice defining themselves and deciding what kind of people they are going to be. In their book about cliques, Charlene C. Giannetti and Margaret Sagarese explain that conforming to the group sends messages to other members that say, "I am a safe, predictable person to be around;" "I am like you;" and "You can trust me."[8]

The Negative Aspects of Cliques

A demand for conformity is typical of many cliques, and while being like one's friends can feel safe and comfortable, it can sometimes interfere with individual decisions and growth. Finding security is positive, but being too afraid to be different is a negative effect of clique membership. In her book, Wiseman interviews fifteen-year-old Gabriella, who talks about her clique and its structure. Gabriella explains,

> My group has rules and punishments about everything. There are seven of us and there can only be seven. I mean, we have kicked people out for breaking the rules and only then can we add someone. We have rules about what we wear. You can only wear your hair up (like in a ponytail) once a week. You can't wear a tank top two days in a row. You can only wear jeans on Friday and that's also the only time you can wear sneakers. If you break any of these rules, you can't sit with us at lunch."[9]

The members of Gabriella's clique could not break or even question the clique's rules without facing unhappy consequences. If they did not conform, they ran the risk of losing their friends. They would be excluded from the group.

Cliques that become exclusive can have damaging effects on classrooms and schools. This is the kind of clique that is often criticized by school authorities, parents, and experts. Such cliques tend to be about popularity and status, and they achieve power by excluding people who are deemed unworthy of clique membership. Group members conform in order to avoid exclusion. People outside the clique may be excluded, not because they do not have interests in common with the group, but because they are not "cool enough" or because they do not have the right kind of material possessions. An exclusive clique makes its members feel special by rejecting anyone not in the clique. It is organized around popularity and is usually ruled by the most popular girl or boy in the class.

Popular Girls' Cliques

Usually boys and girls are in separate cliques. If the popular clique leader is a girl, Wiseman labels her the "queen bee." Wiseman says that this girl is typically pretty and privileged. She does not lead with "good popularity," which Wiseman defines as being liked because she is nice to people. She rules with "evil popularity"—power and control of others. In her clique, the queen bee can be charming and affectionate, and she can get her friends to do what she wants. She is the center of attention

Semipowerful

In her book *Queen Bees & Wannabes* author Rosalind Wiseman says that the most exclusive cliques have a second in command, whom she labels "the sidekick." In a girls' clique, the sidekick is the person closest to the queen bee. The relationship makes the sidekick feel powerful and self-confident. Some of the characteristics of the sidekick are:

Her best friend, the queen bee, tells her what to do, how to dress, and how to think.

The queen bee is her final authority figure, not her parents or school authorities.

She feels as if she and the queen bee are the most important and "everyone else is a Wannabe."

Other people (such as parents) think it looks as if the queen bee "pushes her around."

Rosalind Wiseman, *Queen Bees & Wannabes*. New York: Crown, 2002, pp. 27–28.

The typical "queen bee" rules with "evil popularity"—power and control over others to make them do what she wants.

and controls what happens within the clique. She even controls who can be friends with whom and which girls can be a part of the clique. Other girls admire the queen bee and want to be like her. They want the popularity and importance that being in the clique confers. Wiseman labels these girls "pleasers" and "wannabes."[10] They want to be as powerful and in control as the queen bee, but they also want the security and status that they get from being friends with the queen bee.

Insiders and Outsiders

Exclusive cliques, of course, leave out or reject most of the people in a classroom or grade. So other cliques form in response. Sometimes, for example, there are two popular girls in a class who each form a separate clique and compete for power and status. Other people, who feel rejected and unhappy, form "out-group" cliques, in which they, too, are socially accepted. When Philip Guo joined with the "dorks," he was making a place for himself in a group of his own. In their book *Mom, They're Teasing Me*, Michael Thompson and fellow psychologist Lawrence J. Cohen say that these cliques often choose names for themselves, such as "nerds, dorks, wonks, geeks, brainiacs."[11] Giannetti and Sagarese say that usually about half the class forms friendship circles outside the popular clique. They suggest different categories or stereotypes of these cliques, from "geeks, skateboarders, nerds, and hockey kids to stoners, gangbangers, Abercrombies, Goths, and hootchies."[12] Other popular cliques may be the cheerleaders and the athletes, or "jocks." Of course, the names change as different students choose different descriptions.

BELONGING

"I was def. [definitely] in the theater kid's clique. We weren't freaks, but we were different in a sense…. It made me feel secure about myself."—Dennis, a student at Somerville High School in New Jersey.

Quoted in University of Michigan, "Cool Kids and Losers: The Psychology of High School Students in Peer Groups and Cliques." http://sitemaker.umich.edu/356.tran/testimonials.

Not everyone is a firm member of a clique. Wiseman explains that some people are floaters. Wiseman writes that a floater "has friends in different groups and can move freely among them. She is more likely to have higher self-esteem because she doesn't base her self-worth on how well she's accepted by one group."[13] Floaters have self-confidence, generally are nice to everyone, and do not like conflicts and arguments. Other people in a class may be loners, who are accepted nowhere and have few friends at school. These people are often seen by the various cliques as odd or too different to be accepted. Sometimes, though, they are just newcomers to the school or very shy. Sometimes they are nonconformists who actively reject the idea that they have to fit in to be worthwhile.

As a whole, says Sagarese, social experts have found that middle school students fall into one of four categories. They are "the popular clique, the fringe, middle-friendship circles, or the loners." She explains,

> The popular clique is the cool group—beautiful, charming, affluent, and athletic. They make up about 35 percent of the school population. Fringe kids, about 10 percent of the population, hover around the popular clique trying to get in. The third category, middle-friendship circles, is the largest, with nearly 45 percent of the kids belonging here. Girls in this category form small groups of several friends apiece, and sometimes adopt a style like Goth or grunge. They know they aren't particularly popular. Some care, others don't. The final category is the loner. As [many] as 10 percent of the girls in . . . [a] class sit by themselves in the cafeteria and walk the halls alone.[14]

The Popular Guys

The social experiences of boys mirror that of the girls. Alongside the girls' cliques and outsiders in any grade or class, there are the boys' cliques, although they generally refer to themselves as groups. The popular, exclusive boys' clique also has a leader and followers. Leaders of boys' cliques share similarities with girl leaders, including perceived coolness and popularity. They are respected by other boys and appealing to the girls. Wiseman says the leader of a male clique "is usually the one in the clique everybody wants to be. He's one of or a combination of the following: athletic, tough, able to get the girls, or rich (or able to fake it)." In any class, grade, or school, several boys may earn the title of popular leader. Sixteen-year-old Kevin says, "In my

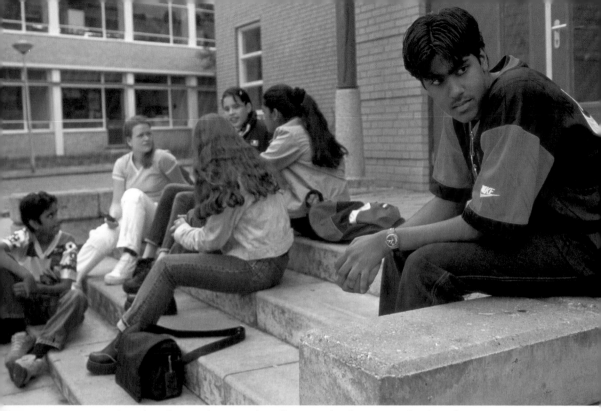

Some boys become loners and totally reject the clique mentality by refusing to conform to any specific peer group.

opinion there can be more than one leader. The leaders can form a clique of their own and have everyone else scrambling, doing anything and everything the leader (s) want them to do."[15]

As with girls, boys' cliques, when they are based on popularity and power, can be exclusive and demand conformity of their members. Some boys are "in" and others are "out." The boys who are outsiders may be those who are smaller than their peers, look different in some way, are unathletic, or have fewer social skills than others. These boys may be rejected and seen as losers. Since popular girls' cliques tend to interact with popular boys' cliques, the male outsiders may be rejected by both groups. Outsider cliques form, giving many boys a place to belong, but, as with girls, some boys become loners and others reject the clique mentality altogether, refusing to conform to any specific group demands. Greg Thomas, for example, hated cliques even during his middle school years. He is an adult now, but he still feels angry about the cliques in his school. He always refused to be a part of one and would not practice exclusion. He remembers, "I had friends who were athletes, intellects, band members, rednecks, potheads, shop kids, disabled, you name it. If you wanted to be my friend, I would be your friend. No one or no group would ever tell me who I could or couldn't be friends with."[16]

Clique Rule Can Be Cruel

Many students, however, do decide who can be a friend based on clique membership. They conform to their clique's rules and traditions by acting in ways that they do not really like or by excluding people outside the group. These outsiders may suffer teasing, taunting, isolation, and loneliness if they have no group where they belong. Different cliques also may engage in competition and conflict. When a class, grade, or school is dominated by cliques, the result is often division, strife, and "us" versus "them" among the various groups. Cliques may seek revenge on one another or struggle to prove which is the most powerful.

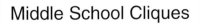

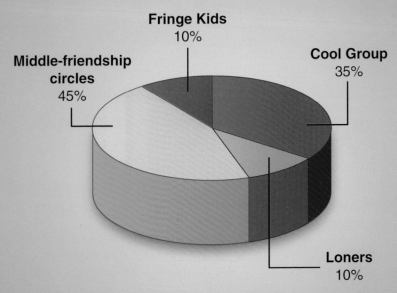

Taken from: www.accessmylibrary.com/article-1G1-113938028/margaret-sagarese-cliques-interview.html.

When an individual takes the "wrong side" in an argument, he or she may be expelled from the clique. Clique members may subject outsiders or former members to ridicule, embarrassment, shunning, or intimidation. Giannetti and Sagarese refer to this situation as a "climate of cruelty," and they report that it is extremely common in schools today.

TRUE FRIENDS?

"These girls are my best friends. I can tell them anything. They'll back me up. But if we're so close, then why do they tease me all the time? If they really are my friends, then why do they make me feel bad?"—Rhoda, age 14.

Quoted in Rosalind Wiseman, *Queen Bees & Wannabes*. New York: Crown, 2002, p. 121.

Middle school students agree that cliques rule in many schools and often can cause trouble. For her book, Wiseman asked sixth-grade girls to write about the exclusive cliques in their grade. These are some of the responses she received:

"In this grade there are cliques and I hate it. Popular people diss people all the time. I know I'm part of a clique, but my clique was formed of all the girls that were excluded and shunned. We like each other for who we are, and not by our hair, looks, clothes, or popularity. These girls are my real friends, no matter what happens."—Michelle, 12.

"I guess, for want of a friend, girls are willing to hurt anyone and don't care what stands in their way."—Kiana, 12.

"There are cliques and even exclusive clubs. There are about three or four cliques and some are nice. The rest are exclusive and mean. Sometimes I feel like I have to conform and be boy-crazy."—Kim, 12.

"I think there are cliques, but we aren't mean to each other mostly. But there are occasional outbreaks of trouble."—Carrie, 12.[17]

The Right Crowd

According to researchers at the University of Michigan, some circles of friends can help people to be successful. For instance, even if the group is not the most popular clique, an academically motivated friendship group can encourage a student to do well in school. Each group member wants to conform, and if that means taking academics seriously, each member strives to perform well in class in order to be accepted. The group influences each member to do his or her best in class.

Group members also learn from one another. If one member is doing extremely well in math, for example, another member may "examine and acquire the other's study habits and tricks for learning the material, thus improving his/her own ways of learning in that subject."

In one 2005 study, researchers discovered that members of an academic group compete with each other but not in a negative way. The members do not try to bring the top student down; instead, they try to figure out "ways to work in order to receive grades similar to the more successful student." Being part of such an academically successful group raises each member's self-confidence and self-esteem, too. "Choosing good friends is like choosing success over failure."

University of Michigan, "Success or Failure: Let Your Friends Pick for You!" http://sitemaker.umich.edu/356 .tran/academic_effects.

Research has shown that academically motivated friendship groups can encourage their members to excel at school.

Trouble from cliques was the subject of a poll of 477 teens between the ages of fourteen and seventeen years old conducted in 2000. According to the poll, 36 percent of the students reported that popular groups practiced intimidation and embarrassment of people not part of their groups "all the time" or "frequently." Another 32 percent reported the same trouble "occasionally." Younger students suffered more problems with embarrassment and intimidation than older teens, and people in rural schools suffered more than those in suburban or urban schools. In addition, about 40 percent of the students reported that nothing happened to the people who intimidated or embarrassed others. They did not get in trouble with school administrators or teachers; other students usually did not object or do anything to stop the behavior; and most victims of embarrassment or intimidation, about two-thirds of them, did not report the trouble at school or at home.

Embarrassment and intimidation, leading to fear and isolation, are the negative impacts that cliques can have on a school's climate and culture. Many educators, psychologists, parents, and students agree that exclusive cliques are a source of serious problems in schools. When cliques get out of control, they can be a major source of teasing, bullying, ridicule, hate, discrimination, and even aggression. Giannetti and Sagarese assert that among many young people there is "a climate where mean-spiritedness is not only accepted but cultivated."[18] And this climate hurts everyone, both insider and outsider alike.

CLIQUES AND SOCIAL CRUELTY

Social cruelty is teasing (including embarrassing, belittling, name-calling, taunting, and insulting), exclusion (including ignoring, rejecting, shunning, and ostracizing), attacking reputations (with gossip, rumors, and lies), and intimidation (bullying and threatening). It is actions and behaviors designed to hurt another person and increase the victimizer's sense of superiority and power. Psychologist Carl E. Pickhardt explains that such social cruelty is "neither innocent nor fun. . . . It is about another person wanting to be mean to you."[19] Many experts believe that exclusive cliques are a major force behind the social cruelty in middle school and high school. It can occur in the classroom, cafeteria, or playground, but it may also go on outside of school during social activities or even on the street. Social cruelty is a phenomenon on the Internet, too, where it is also known as cyberbullying. Clique social cruelty online can be as mean and hurtful as it is in person. Whatever form it takes, social cruelty can be devastating to the victim, disruptive for classrooms and schools, damaging to academic performance, and cause lifelong resentment and regret.

Teasing

Actress Hayden Panettiere was relentlessly teased by fellow students who were in cliques in middle school. She had a hard time making a place for herself and did not fit in because she was different. She was different because she missed a lot of school to act in films, and she thinks that many of her classmates were jealous of her movie success. Panettiere remembers that the popular cliques made her school life miserable. In an interview

In middle school actress Hayden Panettiere faced relentless teasing from her classmates simply because they were jealous of her movie career.

she said, "I was tortured, emotionally tortured by these girls. Every time I came back from filming, it would be me trying to find my way back into the clique. And they weren't having it."[20] Panettiere recalls an incident in the school lunchroom when the popular cliques of both boys and girls played a mean trick on her. She explains, "I remember going to sit with the popular kids for the first time because one girl like invited me over. I was like, 'oh my gosh' and went to sit and one of the guys pulled the chair out from underneath me before I sat down and everyone started laughing. So, I was never the popular girl. Never, never, never."[21] Panettiere was so traumatized by the humiliation at school that she was relieved when she finally graduated from high school and could leave the mean cliques behind her.

BOYS AND GIRLS TOGETHER

"In this class we have the king and the queen, the court, and the commoners."—A fifth-grade boy in California.

Quoted in Jamie Saxon, "Can We Ever Escape Seventh Grade?" *U.S.1*, April 5, 2006, www.princetoninfo.com/index.php?option=com_us1more&Itemid=6&key=04-05-06%20seventh%20grade.

Being different seems to be the primary reason that people are teased in school. Although everyone is teased some of the time, loners and people who do not fit in seem to be continually teased. They may be teased for their clothes, their looks, their body growth and development, their interests, their disabilities, or their behavior—anything that stands out or is different. Matt Lakin went to middle school in the San Francisco area during the 1990s. He remembers that he was an outsider who was teased and called names daily. Because he had long hair and wore casual, scruffy clothing, fellow students singled him out as different. Even in the hallways, people called out to him that he was "stinky" and "smelly." The preppie and jock groups yelled at him to cut his hair. He was even teased for being unusually tall for his age. Lakin says, "Words can really hurt.

A lot of people think it's their job to make people feel bad and they think because they are not hurting you physically that they're not hurting you. But it's pretty emotionally scarring to go through middle school and high school like that and then it makes it hard to go to school."[22]

Name-calling is a common form of teasing. Throughout junior high and high school, Robert Ruane was different from other students because he has Asperger's syndrome, a mild form of autism. Students teased and mocked him for the way he laughed, for acting "weird" and "effeminate" and being inept in gym class. He was called "sissy," "nerd," and "a girl."[23] Fourteen-year-old Gabriela Antonino of Seattle, Washington, was called anorexic because her body was naturally thin. Educator Jane Bluestein describes one female student who was called a cow by the popular groups in her school. Because they were angry at her over a disagreement, they decided to say she was fat. People would make mooing noises at the girl when they saw her, even though she was not overweight. Psychologist Lawrence Cohen says that some of the most common name-calling includes labels such as "stuck-up, bitchy, flat-chested . . . ugly, slut, teacher's pet, tattle-tale, goody-goody . . . sissy, fag, baby, crybaby, mamma's boy, nerd, retard, spaz, fat, [and] shrimp."[24]

Rejected and Cast Out

Name-calling and teasing are forms of bullying and social aggression. Bullying expert Dana Williams says it is not true that "sticks and stones may break my bones but words will never hurt me." She explains, "Words may not break bones, but they can break a child's spirit and self-esteem."[25] Ridicule and name-calling are particularly damaging when a person is teased by a group instead of just one other person because the group also makes a point of excluding their victim. Ruane, for example, was once told that a classmate had invited everyone but him to a birthday party. In another instance, a boy said to him, "Do you ever get the feeling that you're the most hated kid in the school? Well you are!"[26] By the time he reached high school, Ruane had become clinically depressed, was seeing a psychiatrist for help for his low self-esteem, and was sometimes feeling suicidal. Today,

Although name-calling and teasing do not involve physical harm, they are still forms of bullying and social aggression.

as an adult, he blames much of his unhappiness on the rejection and teasing at school and still finds it difficult to forgive the cliques that tormented him.

Clique bullying can take the form of elaborate ostracism and shunning, especially in exclusive girls' cliques. Members of the clique will avoid socializing in any positive way with the victim and target her in a negative way. Young people often call this "outcasting," while professionals may refer to it as "relational aggression."[27] The girls in a clique use relationships to hurt

Little Girls Can Form Cliques, Too

DeAnn Miller-Boschert is an educator and professor at North Dakota State University. She has studied girls' cliques and discovered that sometimes cliques can form at a very young age. When Miller-Boschert was interviewing people for her research, she heard about a preschool where a few four-year-old little girls had formed a club. The children stuck together and refused to let one little girl join their group. In one elementary school, the popular girls formed a plan to let some girls know they were outsiders. Every day, the teacher asked different students to hand out colored pencils to the entire class. Whenever a member of the popular group took a turn, she always gave the prettiest colors to the other girls in the "in" group. She saved the dull, ugly colors for the girls who were "out." Sometimes, an ugly-colored pencil was given to a girl because the popular group was angry at her and wanted to punish her. According to Miller-Boschert, the little girls worried every day about what kind of colored pencil they would have to use.

Child educator DeAnn Miller-Boschert's research reveals that something as simple as colored pencils can be used by young clique members to indicate who is accepted and who is not.

outsiders and exclude them from their social groups. For example the clique leader, or queen bee, may tell her group not to talk to the victim with whom she is angry. The reason for targeting the victim, is not necessarily logical. The victim may have done or said something to upset the queen bee, but she might have done nothing at all. She might be the new girl in school; she could be of a different ethnic group than the clique's leader; or she might be the prettiest girl in the school and seen as a threat. Clique members not only follow the leader's demand but pass it along to fringe members of the clique. These people may not be solid members of the popular clique, but they want to be accepted so they follow along so as to please the clique. Other cliques may join in with the most popular clique's behavior. The popular boys' clique is likely to go along with the members of the popular girls' clique. Quite soon, no one will have anything to do with the victim. No one will talk to her. No one will walk through the halls with her. In their book *Cliques*, Giannetti and Sagarese write, "She's the last one selected for a team in gym. No one will share a microscope with her in biology. She eats her lunch alone. Dirty looks, snide comments, pushes and shoves may add to [her] humiliation."[28]

Gossip and Lies

The victim might also get mean, anonymous e-mails telling her that she is disliked. Rumors may be spread about the victim through the Internet, too. Giannetti and Sagarese describe one situation where everyone at school received e-mails claiming that a thirteen-year-old student was pregnant. It was not true, but many people believed the gossip. Social networking sites, such as Facebook and MySpace, may be used to spread gossip and rumors, too. As this kind of bullying spreads, the victim finds herself friendless and devastated by all the attacks. She is often ashamed and grief stricken, begins to dread going to school or skips classes, becomes unable to concentrate on schoolwork, develops headaches and stomachaches, starts to fail academically, and can develop low self-esteem and self-hatred. The situation is so harmful, say Giannetti and Sagarese, because the victim is "unsure what she did to cause such ill-treatment.

The combination of teasing, gossip, and insults can be so emotionally abusive as to have long-term detrimental effects.

The truth is probably that she didn't do anything." So, it is very difficult for the victim to better her social situation. She becomes a scapegoat, the focus of everyone's aggressive or negative feelings, through no fault of her own. Sometimes, such a victim may turn to alcohol and drugs "to ease her pain."[29]

The combination of teasing, insults, shunning, and gossip can occasionally be so emotionally abusive that it has an extreme effect. Victoria A. Brownworth is a writer and columnist who is still angry about the severe relational aggression she suffered in an all-girls school when she was a teen. She says she was tall and gawky and wore unfashionable clothes because her family was poor. These differences were enough to turn the popular cliques against her. She remembers being "isolated and alone" and bullied every day. She recalls, "There was nowhere to hide from the hierarchy of cliques."[30] Brownworth had no self-esteem and hated her life. She says that the bullying was so bad that she began cutting herself with razor blades and once attempted suicide.

The Harm of Social Cruelty

Clique behavior, no matter how cruel, does not drive all targeted outsiders to suicide, but many experts agree that prolonged social cruelty and relational aggression can be more damaging to victims than overt, physical aggression. JoLynn Carney, a professor of counselor education at Pennsylvania State University explains, "Often the kids with the highest anxiety and depression aren't the kids who are directly abused—punched or called names. It's the indirect aggression, such as spreading rumors and marginalizing a child, that does the most damage." Carney adds that being called names directly is not as damaging as name-calling behind the victim's back. She also says that the silent treatment and shunning are a damaging part of relational aggression. Carney's colleagues, Cheryl A. Dellasega and Charysse Nixon, say that such emotional abuse can lead to "a higher incidence of serious mental health problems such as depression, loneliness, alienation, emotional distress, and isolation"[31] for the victim.

Damaged Bystanders

Clique social cruelty, however, does not just harm the targeted victim. It is damaging for bystanders and even clique members as well. Bystanders are people, whether inside or outside the clique, who do not participate in the emotional abuse but who also do nothing to stop it. Young bystanders are often insecure about their status in the class or school. Giannetti and Sagarese explain, "They resist making waves. . . . There is a big risk in defending a victim."[32] Some of the risks include losing one's friends, being targeted as a victim too, and anxiety that adults will not believe the bystander if he or she reports the abuse.

Giannetti and Sagarese point out, however, that bystanders are not always innocent of social cruelty. They say they are "supporting actors and actresses in our schoolhouse drama" and "assume different roles in clique-land." For example, one kind of bystander may never start a mean rumor about anyone, but he or she is willing to pass the rumor along to others. Another kind is one too involved in his or her own thoughts and activities to think about helping someone else. Another may "play both sides of the fence,"[33] being friendly to everyone and sympathizing with both the victim and the leader. Still other bystanders are genuinely upset when they see someone being cruelly treated. Giannetti and Sagarese say that this kind of bystander often feels guilty, sad, and angry.

By standing around and watching abuse or cruel taunting and teasing, bystanders help support negative clique behavior.

Bystanders do not feel safe in school. If they are members of a clique, they constantly worry that they will be targeted for exclusion if they speak out against clique behavior. If they are outside the clique, they just worry that they will be the next targeted victim. By silently watching abuse or even laughing at cruel teasing or taunting, bystanders help support mean clique behavior and the clique's power. Many wish for the courage to get involved—to confront the clique leader, to walk away, or to befriend the victim—but, because of the power of the clique, they cannot do so.

Damaged Clique Members

Clique members often must worry about being subjected to social cruelty within the exclusive clique. They cannot be sure that their status is secure. Some of the worst relational aggression occurs among clique members. Clique members have such close and intimate relationships that they know each others' secrets. They know how to tease each other in the most hurtful way. They can withdraw the affection and acceptance upon which each member is dependent. In the cool, exclusive clique, membership can be at risk for the smallest transgression, such as dating a boy someone else likes or wearing the wrong brand of clothing.

Wiseman's own personal experience in middle school involved fearful insecurity about losing status within her group. She remembers,

> In seventh and eighth grade, I was part of a powerful clique, but I was at the bottom of the totem pole within that clique. From the outside, I looked like I was popular. From the inside, I felt anything but—my position was incredibly precarious. The girls in my clique teased me all the time. I put up with it because I lived in terror that at any minute I'd be expelled from my group.[34]

Kicked Out

Sudden exclusion from the group is a constant peril for people in cliques. Charlotte Levy was fourteen years old when she lost her clique. She remembers,

It was the first day of ninth grade when my four best friends approached me and told me they no longer wanted to associate with me. In those brief seconds, my world, all that ever had made me happy, crumbled. I was alone, with no one to turn to. I found myself sitting by myself at lunch or, worse, sitting with a group of girls, yet feeling completely invisible.[35]

Charlotte did not know why she had been dropped from her clique, but the experience was terrible for her. She had truly loved the girls in her clique. Her relationship with them had been the most important part of her life. She lost popularity and status, but she also lost her support system, her sense of self-worth, and her sense of belonging in her school.

PAYBACK TIME

"A girl from the 'popular' clique [got] into an accident and had some physical scars from it, including lazy eyes. Her friends would no longer talk to her, and she was always trying to get included into the other cliques. She had been so mean and rude in the past, though, no one wanted to be her friend."—Anonymous.

Quoted in Tammy Swift, "The Secret Life of [Queen] Bees," *NDSU (North Dakota State University)* Magazine, Spring 2005. www.ndsu.nodak.edu/ndsu/news/magazine/vol05_issue02/queen_bees.shtml.

Even group leaders or queen bees may suddenly find themselves deposed and excluded. Psychologists Michael Thompson and Lawrence J. Cohen explain, "Popularity can make you mean, or it can leave you lonely." They say that people who are extremely popular may, as time passes, engender more and more resentment. People can become tired of being intimidated by a mean leader and gang up on him or her. They decide she is stuck-up or he has let his popularity go to his head. Thompson and Cohen say, "Eventually, many of the most popular kids—especially girls—are dethroned by the same group who elevated them in the first place." Then, former queen bees may be cruelly treated, rejected, and isolated. Thompson and Cohen say most people think she is getting "only what she deserves,"[36] if she was mean to others while her status was high. When cliques rule, no one is certain to be safe from social cruelty.

The Damage of Peer Pressure

People in exclusive cliques think that they need to engage in relational aggression to prove their self-worth and do not consider how they damage the self-worth of others. Instead, they feel superior to their victims, even those who are former friends. The popular and pretty queen bee, for instance, is supported in her aggression by other group members who are enjoying the power that seems to increase their own self-worth and status. Everyone follows the clique rules and excludes or bullies those who do not conform. In such a situation, the power of the clique not only hurts outsiders but also, in a strange way, makes group members powerless. They must yield to peer pressure and may lose their independence. Peer pressure is the strong need to behave or think in a certain way so as to be accepted by one's group. One teen, for example, told of being an outcast until he started smoking cigarettes. Then, a circle of smokers accepted him into their group. A young girl found that she was not accepted until she stopped wearing sweatpants to school. When she learned to wear only capri pants, she was allowed to stay in her clique. Popular leaders have to conform, too. Wiseman says they often lose their "real sense of self." She explains that the queen bee "is so busy maintaining her image that she loses herself in the process."[37] The queen bee or popular guy leader must always act cool and self-confident and constantly struggle to maintain his or her status.

Peer Pressure and Risky Behavior

This kind of peer pressure within the clique can lead to a kind of social cruelty within the group. People are afraid to act and think independently, and this can cause members to do things as a group that they would never risk as individuals. The clique members seem to egg each other on. For example, the clique may experiment with drugs and alcohol, engage in shoplifting,

Relational Aggression

The Ophelia Project is an organization dedicated to the understanding and prevention of relational aggression in the lives of girls and women. It defines relational aggression as behavior meant to harm others by damaging or ruining their relationships with other people. According to the Ophelia Project, young people say there are three main reasons that relational aggression is practiced. They are:

Belonging — "If I share the secret she told me with you, my infor-

mation can get me 'in' with the popular group."

Fear — "I'm afraid of being rejected by my classmates, or that I'll be the next target, so I go along with it."

Drama — "I'm bored, and relational aggression creates drama and excitement."

Ophelia Project, "Frequently Asked Questions." www .opheliaproject.org/ main/ra_faq.htm.

or attend unsupervised parties where sexual experimentation is expected. Each group member, including the leader, feels the pressure to look cool to the others and go along with the activity, despite any reservations or discomfort. If a group member does object, he or she may be teased, rejected, or excluded.

Peer pressure does not have to be overt or obvious. In her book, Wiseman quotes fifteen-year-old Sydney who thinks peer pressure is not a problem. Sydney says, "Peer pressure—where there're groups of people pressuring you to do something—doesn't happen anymore. It's not like they say, 'Everyone's doing it, so come on.' People are normally cool with your decision not to drink or do drugs. The only time when you will do it is when you want to fit in with an elite group or you want to impress a guy."[38] Of course, says Wiseman, Sydney does not realize that she has exactly described peer pressure—the need to fit in with the group and impress others.

Peer Pressure and Clique Aggression

Peer pressure is a large part of the problem with cliques. Individuals stop thinking about or taking responsibility for their actions.

Peer pressure plays a part in clique aggression because people stop thinking about, or taking responsibility for, their actions and develop a mob mentality toward others.

Basically good people may ignore their own morals, beliefs, and common sense in an attempt to fit in and impress each other. At its worst, peer pressure within the clique also can result in the group behaving like a mob toward people who do not fit in or who fail to go along with the other clique members. Instead of deciding for themselves, the individuals in the mob act thoughtlessly and destructively in the safety of the crowd. No one has to take responsibility for making the decisions. Clique members may forget their empathy and respect for others. They may torment and relentlessly reject those people perceived as different because "everyone's doing it." This social cruelty can be directed at nonconformers, whether within the clique or outside it.

Relational aggression may not be the only kind of cruelty used by the exclusive clique when people forget empathy and respect. Physical bullying and intimidation of victims may also become a part of the clique's behavior. The group may resort to violence or indulge in overt or anonymous threats. People may get so caught up in the cruel behavior that their actions cause real harm or are even criminal. Many experts lay part of the blame for violence in schools on the culture of cliques.

CLIQUES AND SCHOOL VIOLENCE

Fourteen-year-old Dawn-Marie Wesley lived in Mission, British Columbia, Canada. On November 10, 2000, she used a dog leash to hang herself in her bedroom. By the time her younger brother found her, she was dead. Dawn-Marie left a suicide note for her family in which she explained why she felt she had to kill herself. She had been the target of unrelenting harassment and verbal bullying from a group of three girls. The girls had been Dawn-Marie's closest friends in the past, but Dawn-Marie was now an outsider and victim. In her note, she wrote, "If I try to get help, it will get worse. They are always looking for a new person to beat up and they are the toughest girls. If I ratted, they would get suspended and there would be no stopping them. I love you all so much."[39]

Two Kinds of Violence

Dawn-Marie was not actually physically beaten up, but she was threatened repeatedly. The sixteen-year-old leader of the girls— the "toughest girl"—apparently started the attacks and exclusion because she decided she did not like the way Dawn-Marie laughed. According to Dawn-Marie's mother, the verbal bullying had gone on for nine straight days. The girls threatened to beat up Dawn-Marie or to get other people to do it. One hour before Dawn-Marie committed suicide, she received a harassing cell phone call from two of the girls. One of them directly threatened to kill her and yelled "You are [expletive] dead."[40] Canadian authorities and Dawn-Marie's mother believed that the girl was so frightened and depressed that she thought her only way out was suicide. In an interview, her mother explained,

Ryan Halligan's father believes his son would not have been so severely depressed had he not been bullied by an entire group of people rather than one or two people.

"Well, according to her suicide note, she said that if she didn't kill herself that these girls were going to kill her."[41]

Dawn-Marie's suicide was an act of violence against herself—aggression turned inward instead of outward toward her tormenters. The group of girls, even though they never touched their victim, committed acts of violence, too. Dawn-Marie named the three girls in her suicide note. In a first for Canada's legal system, the girls were charged with uttering threats, and the leader was also charged with criminal harassment. Both are crimes in Canada and in the United States, because the intent to terrorize is considered both illegal and a form of violence. One girl was judged to be more of a bystander and found not guilty. The leader and the other girl, however, were convicted of the charges. It was the first time in Canada that school bullying was legally defined as criminal harassment.

Bullycide: A Form of Clique Violence?

Dawn-Marie is not the only young person to commit suicide because of bullying. Teasing, relational aggression, and physical aggression can all increase the risk of bullycide—suicide caused by relentless bullying and subsequent depression in the victim. This is what happened to Ryan Halligan, a thirteen-year-old boy who killed himself in October 2003. Ryan was bullied by the popular groups of both boys and girls. The boys taunted and teased him and then escalated to physical fights. They spread a rumor, both in school and online, that Ryan was gay. A popular girl that Ryan liked pretended to like him back and encouraged him to instant message with her. Then, she shared his private messages with her group. All of them laughed and taunted Ryan, calling him a "loser" and telling him to his face that his feelings were a joke. Ryan was so humiliated and depressed that he began thinking about and planning suicide. He hanged himself in the bathroom of his home a month after this incident. Ryan's parents say that they know the bullying and ostracism were not the only causes of his death. He was already suffering from depression when he committed suicide. However, says his father, John Halligan, the "bullying and online cyber bullying were significant environmental factors that triggered Ryan's depression. In the final analysis, we feel strongly that Ryan's middle school was a toxic environment, like so many other middle schools across the country for so many young people."[42]

John Halligan believes that Ryan would never have been so depressed if he had been bullied only by one or two people. It was the group ostracism and rejection that overwhelmed him. Psychologist Dorothy Espelage, a professor at the University of Illinois at

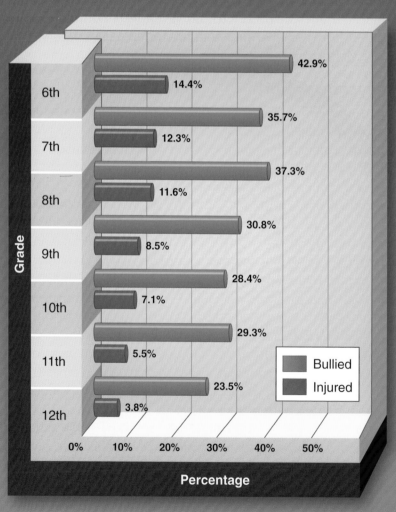

Taken from: Data from Table 11.2 in *Indicators of School Crime and Safety: 2009*, National Center for Education Statistics, U.S. Department of Education (http://nces.ed.gov/).

Urbana-Champaign, agrees with Halligan's assessment. She explains that group attacks are the most common and damaging kind of bullying. She says, "It's groups of kids that do it. Some kids that are popular, this is how they establish dominance; this is how they look cool. Then you've got good kids around them . . . contributing to it, egging it on, not supporting the victim, and ultimately it becomes a climate problem."[43] This is the climate of clique cruelty that can poison the atmosphere and culture of a school.

Violence and Peer Pressure

In almost every school, there are one or more bullies who may act alone and menace others, but bullying with others in a clique can do more harm. The danger is not only bullycide for the depressed victim. Members of a clique—although the members may call themselves only a "club" or "group of friends"—may develop a culture of violence to prove their status to each other. This is not the violence turned against self like suicide but the violence of physical aggression. Wiseman says that this is a particular problem for some boys' cliques. She explains that teenage boys have a need to prove their masculinity to each other. They are especially worried about being labeled as gay or acting like a girl. "Gay," she says, "is the worst insult boys can use against one another and is used whether the target is gay or not. In order to avoid the label, boys may participate in violent behaviors that are erroneously believed to be 'manly.'" Wiseman further explains,

> Homophobia, manifested in boys' fear of being called gay, . . . [traps] them into being complicit in a culture of violence. One of the best but most disturbing ways I can explain this dynamic is gang rape. The perpetrator not only is the first to rape the girl, but is instrumental in convincing the other boys to participate as well. If they don't, their masculinity and loyalty are questioned. Most boys who would never commit an act of violence like this alone will do it if the alternative is going against the group.[44]

Following the Leader?

As part of a group, boys may also turn violent toward one of their own friends in ways that they would never consider as individuals. This is what happened to Michael Brewer, a fifteen-year-old in Deerfield Beach, Florida. Brothers Denver and Jeremy Jarvis, aged fifteen and thirteen, respectively; fifteen-year-old Matthew Bent; fifteen-year-old Steven Shelton; and sixteen-year-old Jesus Mendez were a group of friends who allegedly got angry at Michael—a member of their group—because of an argument about money. Reportedly, Michael got a video game from Matthew and had not paid for it as he agreed to do. The group confronted Michael outside another friend's apartment on October 12, 2009. They surrounded Michael so he could not escape. Jeremy and Steven were apparently just bystanders who only prevented Michael from leaving. Denver allegedly poured alcohol on Michael. Jesus is accused of using a lighter to set Michael on fire. All the while, Matthew allegedly led and directed the attack and told the other boys what to do.

Michael jumped in the apartment pool to put out the fire, but he was severely injured. He ended up in the hospital, burned over 65 percent of his body. After the incident, all the attackers were arrested, and, according to reports, at first laughed about the attack. Later, the Jarvis brothers were reported to be sorry, frightened, and "tearful . . . especially when talking about the specific incident which led to the injuries of the victim." Jesus was reported to have been remorseful, saying he made a "bad decision."[45]

The terrible attack on Michael by his friends caused a great deal of discussion by experts and the news media as to why it occurred. All the boys who allegedly acted violently were reported to have family problems and perhaps emotional problems. Some people blamed the boys' parents for failing to teach their children to solve problems without violence. However, without the bullying ringleader, some experts wonder whether the attack would have occurred at all. Although Matthew's lawyer denied that Matthew was the leader, the group attack may have been at least partially an example of Espelage's "good

Fifteen-year-old Michael Brewer was doused with alcohol and set on fire by a group of boys.

kids" who yield to peer pressure and follow a dominant bully in a climate of social cruelty. Whether or not Michael's group called themselves a clique, they allegedly behaved just as the worst, exclusive cliques do, and perhaps demonstrate the risk of violence in schools where dominance or "coolness" are important parts of the group culture. In other schools around the country, violence or the fear of violence is not unusual when cliques rule. For example, the San Diego, California, board of education reports that 40 percent of high school students in San Diego County say there are "potential violent cliques at their school."[46]

Victims and Violence

Relational and violent aggression may be instigated by exclusive cliques, but perhaps the biggest and most worrisome risk of violence comes from some of the victims of such cliques. The misery cliques cause may lead to an explosion of violence from those who are rejected, teased, ostracized, and attacked. On April 20, 1999, Dylan Klebold and Eric Harris, two outcasts at Columbine High School in Littleton, Colorado, went to school armed with guns and homemade bombs. The bombs failed to detonate, but, with the guns, the pair began a shooting spree that left thirteen people dead and twenty-one injured before they killed themselves. In videotapes and other records that they left behind, the young killers blamed their actions on the exclusion and bullying they endured at the hands of the popular, high-status cliques. Eric Harris wrote in his journal, "I hate you people for leaving me out of so many fun things. And no don't . . . say, 'Well that's your fault,' because it isn't, you people had my phone #, and I asked and all, but no. No no no don't let the weird-looking Eric KID come along."[47]

Author Melissa Beattie-Moss says that both shooters talked about "their murderous rage against the school cliques—particularly the jocks—whose bullying contributed to Harris and Klebold feeling like social outcasts." Harris complained of constantly being teased about his looks and clothing. Klebold warned that he would make "the stuck-up kids" pay for bullying and taunting him. Although, in the end, the young men killed indiscriminately, their actions caused many experts to argue that the school shootings were, at least in part, a result of "victims who snapped."[48]

School Shootings: Are Cliques to Blame?

Ever since the massacre at Columbine High School, psychologists, educators, and other social scientists have debated whether cliques and their social cruelty are a major cause of school shootings. Psychologists JoLynn Carney and Richard Hazler, for instance, state that shooters are students who "come to believe there is nothing they can do in socially acceptable ways to change the people or the system around them. The turning point for their move to extreme violence may have been finalized by that feeling."[49] Although not all experts lay the blame for shootings on social problems, psychologist Dewey Cornell agrees with this assessment. In addition, he believes that outcasts often react to the teasing and bullying they experience by rejecting mainstream culture. He explains,

> They join rebellious cliques that are attracted to counter-cultural ideas, whether they are beatniks, hippies, or goths. Within these counter-cultural groups some youth are especially vulnerable—more angry, alienated, and depressed than their peers, and more susceptible to friends who encourage them to act out or take revenge. In case after case I have seen youth who discussed the possibility of murder with their friends and were advised to go ahead and do it.[50]

The anger felt by outcasts can have different results in boys than in girls. Girls are more likely to turn the anger on themselves and develop self-hatred, depression, and suicidal thoughts, while boys are more likely to become aggressive or violent.

Charles "Andy" Williams, left, of Santee, California, shot two classmates to death and wounded thirteen others. He had been teased and bullied by classmates.

The massacre at Columbine was but one in a string of shootings by school-age boys that brought the issue of bullying to the attention of professionals and the public. In 2001, for example, fifteen-year-old Andy Williams took a gun to his school in Santee, California. He shot two classmates to death and wounded thirteen others. According to reports, he had been bullied, teased, and rejected by the popular people in his class ever since transferring to Santana High School when his family moved from Maryland to California two years previously. Before the shooting, Andy had told friends about his plans. One supposed friend teased him that he was too much of a sissy to actually do it. Other friends in the outcast group encouraged his hate and made fun of him when he told them what he wanted to do.

After the shooting, Gentry Robler, a sixteen-year-old sophomore at Santana High School, said that he was not surprised that violence had erupted at his school. He said, "There's a lot of hate around here. This is a school that was waiting for something like this to happen."[51] Gentry described the cliques in the school as goths, freaks, dorks, jocks, Mexican gangsters, and white supremacists. He blamed the angry counterculture cliques for encouraging hatred.

SCHOOL SHOOTERS

"I'm not condoning the behavior of boys who fight back violently. . . . What I'm saying is that we have to understand that these boys feel invisible, powerless, and humiliated and have good reason to have no faith in the adults who are supposed to protect them." — Rosalind Wiseman, author.

Rosalind Wiseman, *Queen Bees & Wannabes*. New York: Crown, 2002, p. 196.

Jason McLaughlin, a fifteen-year-old student at Rocori High School in Cold Spring, Minnesota, attended a different kind of school. Counterculture cliques were not common, and Jason's few friends did not encourage any violence. Nevertheless, the young man took a gun to school on September 24, 2003, and

Fifteen-year-old Jason McLaughlin walked into Rocori High School in Cold Spring, Minnesota, in September 2003 and shot two students, killing one.

shot two students. One was killed. Some fellow students who knew Jason blamed the teasing and rejection he suffered at the school. One sophomore, Zach Torborg, explained that Jason was small, nonmuscular, and shy. He had severe acne, as well. Zach added, "He got a lot of stuff from people. You know, no-body would leave him alone. People would call him pizza face and stuff like that [because of] his face."[52] Zach said he had been teased and taunted himself the previous year, and he understood how a person could turn violent from the harassment. Jason had not even shot the people who teased him the most; he had apparently just "snapped" and shot without caring who was hurt.

VICTIM RAGE

"Because of my own experience with vicious in-crowd members, my sympathies lay with Eric Harris and Dylan Klebold [the shooters at Columbine High School]." —Anonymous teen.

Quoted in Charlene C. Giannetti and Margaret Sagarese, *Cliques*. New York: Broadway Books, 2001, p. 29.

Thompson and Cohen have looked at the pattern of school shootings and see them as indicative of a climate of cruelty in modern schools. They say,

> The terrible shootings at Columbine High School, and other high-profile school killings, have revealed to all of us that the social climate of a school affects everyone, at every level. . . . In response to those tragic school-related deaths, we are forced to confront over and over again the dynamics of rejected children, who snap under pressure and react with violence. This violent reaction is often an escalation—an extreme escalation—of mistreatment they experienced themselves at the hands of the group. The violence is usually not committed by a "crazy person" out of the blue. It is usually a statement about what the perpetrator perceives as an intolerable social situation.[53]

No Simple Answers

Despite Thompson and Cohen's certainty about the cause of school violence, however, school shootings are very rare, while clique cruelty is quite common. Most people who are ostracized or bullied do not snap and become violent. Princeton University researcher Katherine Newman has studied school shootings extensively. She says that, since 1970, there have only been about twenty-five "rampage" school shootings in the United States, all

Gangs

Gangs are not the same as cliques. There are similarities, but a gang is an extreme form of a clique. Like cliques, gangs give people a place to belong and can involve tight emotional bonds. However, gangs are even more controlling of members than cliques. Members look upon the gang as family, instead of friends. Gangs depend on secrecy and often engage in violent and criminal activity. They control areas, such as neighborhoods and streets, which are outside of school. Gang members also tend to have trouble in many areas of their lives. They are rebellious at home, often uninterested in academic achievement, and likely to drop out of school.

Gangs are not the same as cliques but rather gangs are cliques taken to the extreme.

carried out by boys. She adds that social cruelty is only one of the factors involved in such extreme violence. She explains that school violence has multiple causes that are necessary but not sufficient for a school shooting to occur. No one can predict with certainty who will become violent, but Newman has identified the factors that must be present for a person to decide to kill. One of these factors is a psychological problem such as mental illness, depression, or a history of family abuse.

Newman calls another major factor "marginalization." That means being pushed to the margins, or edges, of the social group and being treated as an unpopular outsider. When people are marginalized, or feel marginalized, they are outcasts, excluded or ignored and perhaps also bullied and teased. They do

Violent Girls

On June 2, 2009, in Sauk Village, Illinois, seventeen-year-old Mercedes Michaels was the helpless victim of a brutal attack by a group of five girls. The beating allegedly happened because the leader, seventeen-year-old Sarah Kraft and her friend Marcelena Castillo (also seventeen) were angry at Mercedes over a boy. The girls had been Mercedes' best friends before the attack. They ganged up on Mercedes in a local park, held her down on the ground, cut her hair with scissors, burned her face and arms with a lighter, and kicked her. A fifth girl, seventeen-year-old Dusty Miller was apparently part of the plan and, police said, drove the getaway car after the attack. A bystander recorded the whole beating with a video camera. Other bystanders watched the beating but did nothing to

help. Police used the video as evidence in their criminal investigation. The three seventeen-year-olds were arrested and charged as adults for the attack. Two younger girls, who were fifteen and sixteen, were charged as juveniles for their participation in the beating.

Mercedes says she did not fight back because she was afraid the girls would kill her. She was brutalized both physically and emotionally. Mercedes was left with bruises, a concussion, a scarred face, and a lot of fear. She lost her self-confidence and her trust in other people. She was afraid to return to school. After the attack, the girls involved reportedly boasted about it on a social networking site. This is a form of cyberbullying and another way that Mercedes was victimized.

not feel successful or socially accepted. For boys, this often means that they do not fit the stereotype of masculine behavior, body type, or interests. However, says Newman, they are not loners. They do not reject other people, but want to be accepted by the group. She explains, "School shooters are looking to gain the attention and affection of their peers."[54] Many become members of outcast cliques and have at least a few friends to whom they confide their plans.

Marginalization seems to be a critical factor in school shootings. According to a report from the U.S. Secret Service, almost 75 percent of school shooters "felt persecuted, bullied, threatened, attacked, or injured by their peers."[55] Newman says that the popular groups in school make the shooter feel like a "dweebish intellectual or outcast."[56] She says shooters have tried over and over to break into the popular cliques and been rejected. The shootings become an attempt to change their image and feel socially important and masculine. Even talking about shooting plans or dropping hints to peers that something terrible is about to happen can make outcasts feel more socially accepted. Such talk gains attention from others, says Newman. Instead of feeling like a failure or a loser, the would-be shooters start to feel successful in "their long struggle for acceptance" because people listen to them with interest. Newman adds, "Once that strategy begins to work, they have backed themselves into a corner and feel compelled to act, lest they be defined as weak or bluffing."[57]

Would Kinder Schools Make a Difference?

Some experts vigorously disagree with the idea that there is a relationship between violent shootings and exclusive cliques. New Jersey educator Willa Spicer, for example, argues that there is no one pattern that describes all school shooters. She explains, "Jumping to conclusions about that pattern can be very delusional—'Well, all of these kids have been bullied,' but all of them weren't."[58] People have blamed poor parenting; violent video games and movies; uncaring, impersonal schools; the news media; and the American culture for school-shooting incidents. However, psychologist Peter Langman concludes, "These [school shooters] are not ordinary kids who were bullied into retaliation. These are not ordinary kids who played too many video games. These are not ordinary kids who just wanted to be famous. These are simply *not ordinary kids*. These are kids with serious psychological problems."[59]

Newman and other experts agree that someone must have a preexisting, serious psychological problem to become a school shooter, but does that mean that clique teasing and ostracism play no role? Even though there is not one profile that fits all school shooters, most, according to a U.S. Department of Education study, were depressed and felt persecuted. Many experts wonder if those feelings could be lessened by a school atmosphere that is accepting of people's differences. Even if cliques are not the direct and only cause of school shootings, many experts believe they are a contributing factor. Wiseman, for example, says, "If we want to stop boys' violence, schools must create cultures that directly confront the social pecking order and hold bullies accountable."[60]

Thompson and Cohen agree that people who are at risk for committing violent acts, such as school shootings, cannot be identified in advance by using a particular profile, but they argue that such violence can be prevented by changing school cultures and eliminating the climate of cruelty. In addition, a kinder school atmosphere might reduce the instances of bullycide and, at the very least, make school a less-miserable experience for outsiders and outcasts who are different from their peers for whatever reason. Thompson and Cohen say, "We can create a culture in the school that promotes acceptance and inclusion, does not tolerate rejection or neglect, and focuses on the responsibility of bystanders to take a stand against all forms of bullying and meanness."[61] In such a school, exclusion, teasing, and ostracism would not be allowed or acceptable. It would mean the end of much exclusive clique activity. Although some people think this goal is unreasonable, others believe that exclusive cliques need to be confronted and perhaps restricted in all schools.

CAN CLIQUES BE DISCOURAGED?

Cliques are suspected of creating a school hierarchy in which some people are less valued than others. They are a way that students segregate themselves so that they do not socialize with other students who are different. Cliques are believed to be a source of relational aggression, physical aggression, and outright violence. They seem to teach and encourage bullying as a social strategy. They are blamed for creating social barriers among students and encouraging stereotypical behavior. They are reported to cause low self-esteem, insecurity, and sadness or depression for outcasts and loners. In addition, many educators believe that when cliques determine the social system of a school, academic performance cannot be optimal. This occurs because students become less concerned about achievement and more concerned about looks, social status, and popularity. Because of the damage that can be caused by cliques, many people—including students themselves—suggest that cliques should not only be discouraged but also combated and restricted.

Outlawing Inequality

One way to combat cliques is through school policy. Some experts suggest that requiring school uniforms or dress codes is an effective way to reduce clique meanness. Educator Jane Bluestein explains, "In some schools, the real dress code is the short list of designer labels the more powerful cliques require."[62] Whether by personal choice or restricted finances, students who own and wear nonfashionable clothing are rejected in such schools. One ninth-grade girl explains, "You coordinate your wardrobe or do your hair differently, just so you

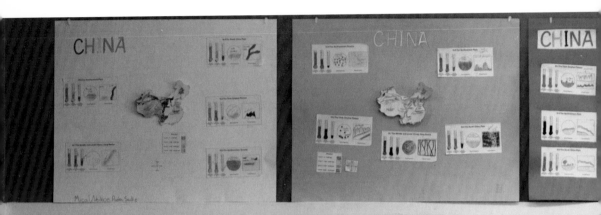

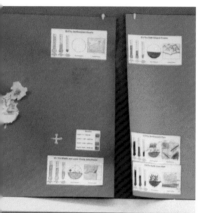

Rigler Elementary School in Portland, Oregon, instituted school uniforms that don't look like school uniforms, basically khakis and blue or white collared shirts.

don't become a victim by being the way you are."[63] The theory behind school uniforms is that this kind of clique discrimination against poorer people or those from different cultures would be eliminated if everyone were required to dress the same.

The debate as to whether required, or mandatory, school uniforms would work to reduce the influence of cliques is a longstanding one. In favor of uniforms, Kalli Gibbs, a high school student in Missouri, argues, "Even though some may oppose it, mandatory use of school uniforms can help transform a school into a safe and unified environment." As part of her reasoning, Kalli says,

> Uniforms will also create equality and uniformity among students and the school as a whole. Schools across the nation are filled with cliques, and for the most part, cliques are usually based on the appearance of the student. Students in uniforms will more easily associate with each other, knowing they are not going to be judged by what they look like on the outside. Uniforms [also] abolish the contest of who's wearing name-brand clothes. Students with economic disadvantages will be less noticeable."[64]

According to Marian Wilde, a writer for the nonprofit educational organization Great

Schools, some of the reasons that educators and experts argue in favor of school uniforms are that they:

- Help students resist peer pressure to buy trendy clothes.
- Diminish economic and social barriers between students.
- Increase a sense of belonging and school pride.
- Improve attendance.[65]

Other educators say that mandatory uniforms discourage the formation of cliques and gangs. This reduces bullying and promotes equality and mutual respect in schools. In 1996 President Bill Clinton said, "If [wearing school uniforms] means . . . our young people will learn to evaluate themselves by what they are on the inside, instead of what they're wearing on the outside, then our public schools should be able to require their students to wear uniforms."[66]

STAYING SELF-CONFIDENT

"I was bullied at school because of my weight and because I used to sing in bands. It started to make me very sharp—I had one-line answers to retaliate. I always had it in the back of my mind that they can say what they want, but I'll always have the last laugh." —Brian McFadden, singer.

Quoted in b-free.ca, "Celebrity Stories."www.b-free.ca/stories_good_company.html.

Clothes Do Not Make the Clique

Some experts believe that if students are unable to evaluate themselves or each other by their clothing, then entire classrooms or whole schools might feel more loyalty and friendliness to all members. Instead of dividing themselves into cliques, the students would accept everyone into their circle of friends. Julia Wilkins is a teacher and writer from England who now works as an educator in the United States. She says, "It is believed that school uniforms enhance students' school spirit and

Critics of school uniforms point to the fact that British students have worn school uniforms for decades but cliques, bullying, and exclusivity are still common.

sense of belonging."[67] Wilkins, however, does not believe that mandatory school uniforms will prevent exclusive cliques and aggression. She explains that in England students have worn school uniforms or adhered to dress codes for decades, and yet, cliques, bullying, and exclusivity are common. She says that requiring the same-colored clothing (for example, white shirts with blue skirts or pants) does not really mean there are no differences in clothing. Some outfits will be more expensive than

Does the Punishment Fit the Crime?

In 2005 a teacher in one Manitoba, Canada, school decided to punish a group of four elementary school boys for bullying their classmates. The teacher made the boys wear hockey helmets that were labeled with "Loser," "I tease people," and "I'm stupid because I am a bully." Then the boys had to sit in front of the class while other students criticized and teased them. The teacher's actions caused a lot of controversy in Canada. Some people who heard of the punishment thought it was a good way to stop bullying. Others, including some parents, said the treatment was little more than bullying by the teacher.

CBC News Online, "Sticks, Stones and Bullies," March 23, 2005. www.cbc.ca/news/background/bullying.

others. Some may be newer or cleaner than others. Uniforms and dress codes, Wilkins argues, do not erase differences among people.

As to wealth and status determining who is popular and who is rejected, Wilkins says these factors cannot be hidden by wearing uniforms. Students know anyway who has money and privilege. Exclusive cliques cannot be stopped by trying to pretend that everyone is equal in all areas. Wilkins explains,

> I know from growing up in England, where until recently school uniforms were mandatory, that children are acutely aware of each other's social and economic status, regardless of uniformity of school attire. School uniforms can do little to disguise socio-economic status. As the choice to wear designer clothing often has more to do with priorities than wealth, and the fact that both the richest and poorest members of society can be seen wearing brands such as Tommy Hilfiger and Nautica, clothes can no longer be an indicator of social class. Accents, grammatical usage, values, leisure pursuits, and general lifestyles are often more revealing indicators.

If students are to be prepared for the outside world, they need to be prepared for a world riddled with inequalities, injustices, and inflexible social divisions. Attempting to equalize everyone by pretending these divisions do not exist doesn't eradicate the problem; it merely disguises it.[68]

Rejecting Rules

Many experts agree with Wilkins's assessment. Dress codes or uniforms imposed by schools can never eliminate the problems of exclusive cliques. Not only may students resent being told what to wear, but they are also prevented from expressing their individuality. Students may resist rules about how they can dress. In 2006 researcher and professor David J. Jamison studied sixth-grade students in one southern U.S. school where a new dress code policy had been instituted that year. In this school of 650 students, following the dress code policy was not mandatory. However, the school strongly encouraged and urged students and parents to choose uniform colors for pants, shorts, skirts, and shirts. To determine how the students reacted, Jamison studied the students for one entire school year. He asked 118 students to write essays about their personal clothing choices and why they were important. He handed out survey questions to all the students asking for their opinions of the school uniform policy. He kept track of how many students actually wore school-recommended outfits.

Jamison's results suggest that the majority of students did not like the school dress code. At the beginning of the school year, 70 percent of the students were following the dress code. By the end of the year, fewer than 20 percent of the students did so. In one of Jamison's surveys, 307 out of 466 students "expressed disapproval of the uniform policy." In their essays, some students agreed that uniforms could increase a "sense of pride" and encourage "team spirit" at school. They said that the policy "makes everyone appear equal." Even those who disliked the dress code recognized that it reduced the pressure to buy expensive clothes. Many students reported, however, that people still wanted to dress like the others in their cliques, usually in expensive brand-name clothing. Even wearing uniforms did not stop people from inventing styles that identified them as members of certain cliques. For example, the "very handsome, athletic"[69] leader of the most popular boys' clique began wearing argyle socks with his uniform. Soon, all the members of that clique wore argyle socks that identified them as clique members. Jamison says clique identification does not depend on certain brand-name clothing. In other studies in other schools, he reports that students use brands of athletic shoes, hairstyles, baseball caps worn between classes, shoes kept unlaced, or even too-large uniforms in order to indicate clique membership.

Jamison theorizes that clothes "are among the most important symbolic representations of group identity and belongingness within the subcultures of late childhood–early adolescence in the US."[70] Even with mandatory school uniforms, many experts agree that students will find a way to use other symbols (hair, shoes, and so on) to show that they belong to a certain clique, and, they argue, cliques cannot be prevented with rules about school uniforms.

Cliques Are Here to Stay

Eddie Baumann, a professor of education at Cedarville University in Iowa, warns, "Cliques are a part of middle school life. Regardless of how well-meaning we may be as adults, we cannot eliminate them." Baumann says that cliques cannot be prevented because he recognizes the benefits of belonging to a group. He knows that students will always seek out friends with common interests and attitudes who can provide emotional support. However, Baumann and other experts do believe that the negative aspects of cliques can and should be controlled. Baumann says that "avoiding the ugly" side of cliques is the responsibiltiy of parents and school authorities, with the help of the students themselves. To control the negative side of cliques, he recommends supportive and caring school environments in which students know the rules and feel safe. He explains,

> These are environments that caring, supportive adults develop and maintain. Expectations are reasonable, rules

Cliques are part of school life and cannot entirely be eliminated because there are positive benefits to belonging to a group that shares common interests.

are minimal, and the rules that exist are understood as mutually beneficial [helpful for everyone] and not controlling. Adults model compassion, care, and justice to all students by defending victims of attacks or cruelty. They also provide emotional and, at times, institutional support for students who take the risk of defending those who receive unjust treatment.[71]

Caring Schools, Caring Students

Giannetti and Sagarese say that tolerance, empathy, and respect are the best ways to fight the relational aggression, bullying, violence, and exclusion that represent the negative side of cliques. Schools that help students to develop these caring, inclusive attitudes usually make everyone feel "valued and important." Many different schools around the country have instituted such "clique-busting programs." In Long Beach, California, for example, school authorities helped the girls in one middle school to form a club called "Circle of Friends."[72] The club had five hundred members. Its goal was to reach out and make friends with anyone who was not in a popular clique or who was unhappy with the actions of their own cliques. The club members wore friendship bracelets and signed pledges to include anyone in the group who wanted to join. They agreed not to tease or attack anyone for his or her looks, clothing, body type, interests, or differences. The club was successful in reducing bullying and ostracism because the members were accepting and inclusive toward everyone at the school. By supporting student efforts and promoting a school atmosphere of kindness and respect, the teachers and the administration made it possible for students to reject exclusion and stand up for each other.

Students need the support of the school faculty in order to fight the meanness and aggression that can result from exclusive cliques. They need to know that school faculty will act if they are threatened or bullied for defending clique victims and that they will not become victims of cruel clique attacks themselves. Giannetti and Sagarese say that students can take charge of clique busting with just a little help from caring teachers. They explain,

> At Shenendehowa High School in Saratoga County, New York, students invented The Respect Club. The club had a faculty advisor and guidance from the local teachers' association, but the students were in charge. Members took an "I choose respect" pledge. They signed a card promising to tell an adult if they heard of any potential violence. . . . The club had an escort service made up of volunteers who accompanied a frightened or victimized student to class.

The school allowed the club members an "annual day" when they could talk to the whole school about the value of a "civil, dignified, and supportive way of treating one another." They talked about their goals of "reducing discrimination and peer-to-peer harassment." The school faculty helped by offering annual awards for outstanding efforts in "the respect department."[73] Negative clique behavior was dramatically reduced.

Sometimes, a small change in school rules can make a big difference. When Richard Wendell Fogg was the principal of a junior high school in Washington, D.C., he decided to try to put a stop to the name-calling and put-downs that he heard from students. He talked to the students in his school about how cruel such relational aggression can be. He recounted his own experiences in the marines. He described how demeaning it was when his drill sergeant attacked him with nasty put-downs. He explained that he was hearing the same kind of insults and hurtfulness at his school. Then he started a very simple program: Whenever any student heard someone insult or put down someone else, the bystander had to say, "We don't do that here."[74] The atmosphere of the school changed, and the slogan was adopted by other schools and groups that needed to fight exclusive cliques and bullying. One group even added another part to the slogan program. Any

School faculties can help minimize the negative effects of cliques by establishing programs that reduce discrimination and peer harassment.

person who insulted someone had to apologize and give two compliments to the person he or she attacked.

How Students Can Fight Cliques

Giannetti and Sagarese say, "The best way to eliminate cliques and bullies is to encourage the silent majority to speak up. Those kids who stand on the sidelines, watching other children

How Targets Can Discourage Bullying

Victims of bullying and teasing can empower themselves by knowing some practical ways to respond. Debra Piotrowski and James Hoot are bullying experts with some suggestions. They write,

- Ignore the bully's behavior whenever possible.
- Use social skills, such as being assertive, negotiating, sharing, taking turns, inviting others to participate, assisting others, and asking for permission.
- Leave the situation.
- Rebuff in a firm manner.
- Protect yourself emotionally and physically (without using retaliation).
- Request that the bully stop, and then walk away; if this does not work, then tell the teacher.
- Use humor.
- Own it (the criticism) by pre-

tending to agree with the bully (this takes the power away from the bully).
- Spend time in groups.
- Practice what to say in front of a mirror or with friends.

What Not to Do:
- Cry or act hurt in front of the bully.
- Lose your temper.
- Escalate the situation.
- Return the aggression.
- Get others to gang up on the bully.
- Tease in retaliation.
- Call the bully names.
- Bring weapons to school.

Debra Piotrowski and James Hoot, "Bullying and Violence in Schools: What Teachers Should Know and Do." www.thefreelibrary.com/Bullying+and+violence+in+ schools%3a+what+teachers+should+know+and...- a0184799384.

be humiliated, hold the key to reform in their hands."[75] By-standers are almost always in the majority in a class or school, but speaking up takes a lot of courage and self-confidence. Principal Fogg helped bystanders to fight clique meanness with his slogan of "We don't do that here," but there are ways that bystanders can respond without adult help, especially if they can get other students on their side.

Some of the tactics that Giannetti and Sagarese suggest are:

Don't watch. The clique leader wants an audience. Don't give her one. Walk away.

Don't react. If it's not possible to leave, . . . refusing to laugh or endorse the clique leaders' action with words may shut him down.

Don't gossip. Passing on rumors—in notes, whispers, or emails—can hurt feelings and may even escalate the conflict to violence.

Offer verbal support in private. [Talk with the victim and let her or him know someone cares and disagrees with the bully.]

Gather others. A clique leader will have a more difficult time tormenting someone if several kids in the class leap to the [victim's] defense.

Extend an invitation. [Reach out and be a friend. Invite the excluded victim to go to the movies or come for a visit.]

Start an online support group. [Invite a victimized person] to join in a chat or instant messaging session. Once kids talk together online, their friendships often spill over into the classroom.

Get a teacher involved. If the action occurring is violent, . . . opt for grabbing the nearest teacher.

Confront the bully. [Object to what the bully is doing but only if it is safe, and the bully cannot retaliate. Make sure a teacher is nearby in case help is needed.][76]

"Mix It Up"

Some schools have tried very creative programs to reduce relational aggression and exclusion. They encourage students to broaden friendships and social interactions, thereby, it is hoped, increasing tolerance, empathy, and respect. These programs require student participation instead of leaving it up to individuals to try to change clique behavior. Many students, even those in cliques themselves, seem to appreciate such school efforts.

WINNING IN THE END

"Be nice to nerds. Chance's are, you'll end up working for one."—Bill Gates, founder of Microsoft.

Quoted in Jane Bluestein, "Pretty and Popular," JaneBluestein.com. www.janebluestein .com/articles/popular.html.

At Powell Middle School in Brooksville, Florida, for example, students participated in Mix It Up at Lunch Day in November 2008. For one day, students did not eat lunch with their cliques or groups. No one sat alone, either. Above each table, teachers posted different quotes. One quote was from India's former prime minister, Indira Gandhi. It read, "You cannot shake hands with a clenched fist." As the students came into the cafeteria, they were handed a piece of paper with one of the quotes on it. They sat at the table that matched that quote and found more pieces of paper. These contained "ice breaking"[77] questions to ask and answer to help them get to know each other. Students shared information about their families, favorite sports or music, and hobbies and interests. The idea was to help students become more accepting and understanding of each other and perhaps even make new friends outside their cliques.

A National Movement for Kindness

Mix It Up at Lunch Day is part of the national Teaching Tolerance project developed by Morris Deeds, the founder of the Southern Poverty Law Center. Teaching Tolerance is a program for teaching tolerance, fighting prejudice, and creating school inclusiveness instead of clique exclusion. Its goal is "to break down the barriers between students and improve intergroup relations so there are fewer misunderstandings that can lead to conflicts, bullying, and harassment." In 2008 about 3 million students in more than eight thousand schools in the United States had a Mix It Up at Lunch Day. According to Teaching Tolerance, "The event is a simple call to action: take a new seat in the cafeteria. By making the move, students can cross the invisible lines of school division, meet new people and make new friends. Mix it Up at Lunch Day helps students become more comfortable interacting with different kinds of people."[78]

Mix It Up at Lunch Day is most successful when both teachers and students work together to make it happen. Teaching Tolerance says, "By working together, students and teachers can create real change."[79] At Blanchard Middle School in Westford, Massachusetts, for instance, administrators, teachers, and students join together to make their day worthwhile. Classes are suspended for the day so that people can talk about the value of their experiences. Students sit at cafeteria tables with assigned numbers instead of eating with their friends. Eighty-eight percent of students report that they believe these days are worthwhile. The principal of the school explains, "At first, some students didn't want to sit with others they aren't friends with. But after lunch, some new friendships had been made."[80]

Teachers help by conducting workshops and activities during which students can talk about the lunch period and its meaning. They discuss what makes a good leader and the value of positive communication with others. They increase their trust in each other with an activity in which a blindfolded student is led through an obstacle course by another student. They learn to determine their own self-esteem (instead of relying on clique standards) by writing stories about themselves that describe their positive qualities.

Embracing Diversity, Ostracizing No One

The Teaching Tolerance project suggests several activities that can reduce clique aggression and promote tolerance. One activity helps students to recognize and question their own prejudices about people outside their comfortable groups. In this activity, students examine and define their stereotypes and possible homophobia by filling out a form with words that describe male athletes, female athletes, male artists, and female artists. "Strength" and "manliness" might be written for male athletes, for example, as positive qualities. The same words might be negative for female athletes because of assumptions students have made that these women are not feminine or are gay. "Sissy" or "gay" might be used to describe a male artist but not a female artist. Students discuss whether homophobia is based on stereotypes. They question the truth of these stereotypes. They talk about how to get rid of the stereotypes that lead to teasing and ostracism in their school. As a group, they try to develop a plan to combat stereotyping and homophobia.

Teaching Tolerance recommends similar activities for fighting racial prejudices (such as eating lunch only with people of one's

Students at Warren Hills Middle School in Washington, New Jersey, participate in Mix It Up at Lunch Day as part of a national Teaching Tolerance project for teaching tolerance, fighting prejudice, and creating school inclusiveness.

Morris Deeds, cofounder of the Southern Poverty Law Center and Teaching Tolerance project, talks with students in Alabama during a Mix It Up event at their school in 2007.

own race), social status prejudices, (such as devaluing people who are poor and unable to buy expensive clothing), and religious prejudices (such as avoiding and ignoring people whose religion is different). All of these discussions and activities are designed to help people accept diversity and practice inclusion in schools. With attitudes of tolerance, kindness, and respect, students can minimize the damage caused by cliques. They recognize that clique teasing, bullying, and exclusion are based on a kind of bias or prejudice, and they commit to ending those attitudes and learning to be comfortable with differences. They do not have to give up their social groups; they just become willing to add to their lists of friends.

SOCIETY AND THE DEVELOPMENT OF CLIQUES

A merican middle schoolers and high schoolers are not the only people who have to cope with and make decisions about exclusive cliques. Around the world, especially in wealthy countries, cliques can be a problem for young people, and clique-like behavior may exist at all ages and in all cultures. Some people blame the formation of cliques on the attitudes and structure of society itself.

Cliques in the UK: Still About Discrimination

Cliques are as common in the United Kingdom as they are in the United States. Brand names and labels are just as important to British students as they are to American students and are often used to distinguish clique membership. Students pick on those who are different, whether the difference is upper class versus lower class or another difference such as race, disability, or looks. Educator Julia Wilkins says, "Bullying has been going on forever in British uniformed schools."[81] British schools no longer require uniforms, and so unfashionable clothing is as big a problem in some schools as it is in the United States. Luke Jackson, a British young man, has written about the bullying he has seen in England. He says his older brother, Matthew, had a big problem with bullies the year he started high school. A group of boys in Matthew's class began teasing him unmercifully because of his winter coat. The coat was a low-priced, practical, plain brown coat that his mother had bought for him.

The boys called Matthew "earthworm Jim" because of the color and finally attacked him and tore his coat. The teasing over clothing stopped only when Matthew's mother bought him a name-brand, "trendy"[82] jacket.

The right clothing, however, could not stop the teasing and bullying that Luke himself endured. He has Asperger's syndrome and does not have normal social skills. He believes that popular groups attack people they consider "soft." Luke, for example, was

When British schools stopped requiring school uniforms, bullying over not having the right clothes increased.

unathletic, unwilling to fight anyone, and uninterested in typical male pursuits. At his first school, Luke was targeted and victimized by a group of four boys for several years. Luke remembers, "They used to push me and shove me and call me names and generally try to make my life miserable. Those four boys in particular seemed to make it their lifelong mission to annoy, upset, hurt, and aggravate me."[83] Luke did not escape the persecution until his mother withdrew him from the school and enrolled him in a private school. Cliques and bullying were not unknown at that school, either, but at least the students were more worried about getting in trouble and being reported to their parents because their parents were more involved at the private school. Luke was no longer a perpetual victim.

A Clique by Any Other Name . . .

British private schools, however, have their share of cliques; they are just based on different standards than those in the United States. Instead of jocks, geeks, cheerleaders, and so on, British groups may refer to themselves and others as "posh," "chav," "emo," or "gorm." Posh students, for example, are "preppie" and proud of their money and privilege. They are seen to be in a higher social class than other students. Chav students are seen as tough, sometimes wild, delinquent types who are members of the working class. Gorms is a put-down used by popular people that means clueless losers, and emos are emotional people who like a certain kind of punk rock music. The labels may be different, but the stereotypes have the same effect: exclusion of people outside one's group and increasing one's own status by victimizing or ostracizing others.

British teen Jade Prest became a victim when a rumor swept through her school that she had slept with her friend's boyfriend. According to Jade and her mother, the rumor was begun by one ringleader and her gang in order to ostracize nonconforming Jade. Soon, everyone at school was whispering about her and calling her names. The bullying escalated to prank phone calls, threatening text messages, and mean gossip about her on Bebo (a social networking site). A new rumor spread that she was a drug addict.

Jade was cyberbullied so severely that people became afraid to be seen with her or talk to her. Former friends dropped her out of fear that they would be attacked next if they supported her. Jade became isolated and very unhappy. She lost confidence in herself and trusted no one. She remembers, "Things got so bad I didn't even feel like myself anymore. There was nothing I could do to get them off my back. In the end, I was trapped in my own home. It was like a prison."[84]

Jade began to avoid friends. She would not go to the movies or even walk down the street for fear of harassment. She stopped using the Internet. She panicked every time her phone rang. She stopped going to school. She began to suffer with depression. Finally, she attempted suicide. Fortunately, her life was saved, and Jade transferred to a new school. She graduated from high school in 2006 and has made a good life for herself, but she still says that she will never forget the bullying.

An Ostracism Epidemic

Val Besag, a British educational psychologist says that Jade's story illustrates, in an extreme way, an epidemic problem in Britain with girl cliques and bullying. She explains, "Boys have a hierarchy based on physical power, girls have a hierarchy based on friendships. . . . When girls bully, it can be more distressing because the attack is emotional and involves social exclusion."[85] Whether they call themselves a gang, a clique, or a friendship group, and whether they use physical or relational aggression, the students of the UK seem to live with the same meanness and exclusiveness that American students do.

Phil Beadle, a British teacher, argues that discrimination and prejudice are epidemic in school social groups in Great Britain. He attempts to encourage inclusive behavior and tolerance for differences with a large bulletin board in his classroom. The title on the bulletin board reads "Acceptable Versions of Masculinity." Underneath he includes "pictures of billionaire geeks; cross-dressing athletes; transvestite comedians; disabled, Irish, punk shouters; transsexual models; and (reputedly) gay footballers." Beadle adds, "It has been the springboard for much discussion."[86]

Is It Better in Austria?

Philipp Aschauer is a college student in Austria who has written a blog comparing the cliques in American high schools with the Austrian school experience. He argues that the Austrian school system is so different from the U.S. system that exclusive cliques are not a problem in his country. He says that the American system of moving students through different classes throughout the day forces students to form social groups in order to find a way to fit in and belong.

In Austria, the school system keeps students grouped together as one class. Aschauer explains,

> We all have them, emos, punks, alternative kids, nerds, but they are all physically gathered in one class. Forming a class with all kinds of people requires you to put up with people

of different interests and sooner or later you develop a common sense of community. You realize you can't just ignore them, because even during breaks, you have to deal with them. After one class is finished you don't usually flee out of the class room but you get out your lunch package and socialize with those who are around you.[87]

Still, Aschauer recognizes that exclusiveness can occur in Austrian schools, too. He explains, "Of course, there are more popular kids than others and single students get excluded from groups in Austria too, so one cannot say that cliques are a US

In Austria students are grouped into the same class all day. This encourages students to interact with people who are different and makes it harder to form cliques.

Girl Clubs

In Queensland, Australia, in 2008, the principal of Mackay's St. Patrick's College (equivalent to a U.S. private high school) made a disturbing discovery. A small group of teen girls had formed a special club (a clique) that they called Club 21. To be in the club, a girl had to be thin, pretty, and popular.

Each girl in the club was ranked by the others according to her weight, her looks, and how appealing she was to boys. Many of the girls wore their "number" on their wrists. Apparently, numbers got higher if the club members engaged in binge drinking or sexual activity. The girls excluded and looked down on anyone not part of their club.

According to Australian educators, popular, exclusive clubs are common in Australian schools, both public and private. The club members tease, gossip about, and bully girls who are not a part of their group. Educators in Australia report that three out of every five girls in Australian schools are teased about their looks or clothing.

Although most Australian students do not belong to a popular club, almost all girls say they exist in their schools, and many have been hurt by them. The girls who are not "in" often suffer a loss of self-confidence and a fear of being victimized. Educators say the clubs pose a risk for their members, too. The clubs encourage dangerous behaviors such as eating disorders, alcohol abuse, and sexual promiscuity.

American phenomenon only."[88] Students in Austria may be forced together enough that their cliques are less rigid and isolating than in America or the UK. However, cliques still exist, and popularity remains an important issue for some students. The cliques may not be based on ethnic groups or alternate lifestyles, but they are not completely inclusive either.

Religion, Race, and Cliques

In Malaysia, race and religion seem to play a large role in the formation of cliques at schools. Unlike in U.S. schools, however, students appear comfortable in inclusive groups while they are in high school and middle school. Only as they get older do cliques based on race and religion become important. Malaysia is a multiracial, multicultural society. Researcher Timothy P.

Daniels reports that non-Malay students, such as Chinese, Indian, and Portuguese young people, tend to form friendship groups that are often separate from the Malay or Malay and Indian friendship cliques.

Daniels says that these students all got along when they were younger, but as they grew older, that changed. Differences in religion and society's treatment of the different ethnic groups may be the cause of this change. For example, as Malay girls get older, they begin wearing *tudung* (Islamic headscarfs), and this symbol sets them apart from non-Malay classmates. Young males may wear special hats to identify themselves as Malay. Non-Malay students may tease and ridicule their classmates for their Muslim clothing. Malay students say that, as the differences grow, Chinese students sometimes act superior and refuse to associate with them.

Society itself adds to the problem. Because of a quota system based on ethnicity, Malays are allowed into colleges with lower grades than non-Malays. Parents may encourage their children to drop their non-Malay friends because of disapproval of interracial or mixed-religion future marriages. Many non-Malays believe that Malays get the most privileges, both in and out of school. In Malaysia, says Daniels, cliques are not about who is included and who is excluded. They are "a combination of the two."[89] Individuals are not isolated and ostracized by everyone; instead, they are included by some groups and excluded by others.

School Biases and Discriminatory Cliques

Malaysia is not the only place where school cliques and discrimination seem to be based on the attitudes of the society as a whole. Educator Jane Bluestein believes that popular cliques are supported and sometimes encouraged by the prejudices of school officials and teachers. She argues that bias and discrimination is common and most often based on social class, appearance, clothing, and athleticism, particularly in wealthy countries. As an example, Bluestein describes the experiences of one high school girl who knew she was favored in school because she was well-to-do and academically gifted. She was allowed to leave school in her car during the lunch hour while other students were not. She noticed that the "rich kids" all took

As they get older, students in Malaysia tend to form cliques based on race and religion.

gifted classes, participated in student government, and were involved in sports. The poorer people were left out. This girl said, "It made the poor kids hate the rich kids even more."[90]

Another high school student told Bluestein about the favoritism teachers displayed toward the "jock culture." The student remembered an incident when a popular cheerleader was late for geometry class. She got only a warning, but two other non-athletes in the class were given detentions that same day for the same offense. Bluestein also reports the conclusions by a group of researchers that "teachers, particularly male teachers, often sided with student athletes accused of harassment, especially sexual," and defended and gave advice to these students about how to avoid trouble. Bluestein says students are reported to experience classroom discrimination from teachers because of their appearance, too. Several students told her about teachers ridiculing and making jokes about certain hairstyles and outfits. One girl told about being treated by teachers as "a menace to society"[91] because she dressed in black outfits and wore steel-toed boots.

In a study conducted by researcher Richard Arthur, some school gang members were asked to dress "straight." Arthur persuaded them to come to school wearing coats and ties. He found that teachers' attitudes changed dramatically. They treated the boys with respect and "commented on what good looking young men they were."[92]

LEARNING EXCLUSION

"We teach children how to discriminate every day. By defining people by their skin color, ethnic background, intelligence, sexual preference, geographic origin, or religious beliefs, we show children how to perceive the world through the lens of an 'us' and a 'them.'" —Michael Thompson and Lawrence J. Cohen, psychologists.

Michael Thompson and Lawrence J. Cohen with Catherine O'Neill Grace, *Mom, They're Teasing Me*. New York: Ballantine, 2002, p. 166.

Bluestein's and Arthur's observations suggest that students cannot be expected to practice tolerance, acceptance, and respect if adult society does not. When the school culture practices discrimination, it is no wonder that students find themselves drawn to exclusive cliques. Bluestein proposes that they are just mirroring the larger society when they reject, isolate, and ostracize people. She says to teachers, "You can't just stand up in a room and say, 'Now kids, we are going to do a lesson on respect. Now respect is important because "yada yada" and let's put some posters on the wall.' This doesn't work, especially in an environment where teachers speak so disrespectfully to kids and to one another. How often are we not walking the talk?"[93]

Egypt's Schools

In Egypt, says writer Catherine C. Harris, cliques are nonexistent. She explains, "Everyone [in a class] just hangs out together as a big group, and there are no small groups that form their own private clique." Harris believes this difference between American schools and Egyptian schools is a result of school structure.

In Egypt, each group of students in a particular grade stays together in one classroom all day. It is the teachers who rotate among different classrooms, not the students who change classes. Harris says, "Some students say that this is boring, to stay in the same classroom all day, but the positive outcome is that the students become better and closer friends within that class." The system makes for a more inclusive school experience.

Catherine C. Harris, "Children in Modern Egypt," Tour Egypt, September 27, 2005. www.touregypt.net/feature stories/children.htm.

In Egypt each group of students in a grade stay together in one classroom all day.

Discrimination, Exclusion, and Parents

Thompson and Cohen agree that adults can encourage the discrimination that leads to exclusive cliques, but they argue that parents play a large role. For example, parents may gossip about other parents and teens in front of their own children. They may form circles of friends that snub outsiders. They may leave out some of their child's classmates when throwing a birthday party, perhaps because they are of a different race or because they are poor. Thompson and Cohen say, "A school that has a problem with cliques among the students often has cliques among the parents as well. Queen bee daughters often have queen bee moms, who may exclude other parents from their in-group."[94] In addition, parents may interpret what happens in schools in different ways. One parent, for example, might be upset by the bullies in a classroom; another parent may complain that a son or daughter is exposed to a "weirdo" in the classroom who does not fit in.

Giannetti and Sagarese argue that most adults have prejudices that they need to recognize and fight. Such prejudices may be based on social class, race, homophobia, or even disability. Young people learn intolerance from their parents, and their classrooms become a "microcosm of society" because clique cruelty is "based on intolerance for others."[95] In the world of the classroom, students act on and imitate the prejudices they have learned at home and in the larger world. In one study by the National Science Foundation and the National Institute of Mental Health, scientists found that 90 to 95 percent of all adults have prejudices, even though they may not be aware of them. Does this mean that attempts to stop the cruelty of exclusive cliques are doomed? Giannetti and Sagarese say no. They believe that most people want to change and become more accepting. First, people have to recognize their prejudices, and then they have to practice tolerance in what they say and how they act. The researchers believe that children and teens will become more tolerant, inclusive, and accepting if their parents do.

Society's Climate of Cruelty

Some experts argue, however, that even perfectly tolerant and accepting parents and teachers are not enough to stop the climate of cruelty caused by school cliques. Social worker William Voors says that the whole of U.S. society is less civil and polite than it was in the past. People are exposed to vulgar language, demeaning jokes, and prejudiced insults and seem to see such behavior as normal or acceptable. Voors asserts, "Harassment, malicious teasing, and bullying happen in boardrooms and schoolrooms, on school buses and factory floors, in school and office hallways, and email chat rooms." Because ugly, cruel behavior is part of the culture, young people are unaware that such actions are harmful and not okay. They imitate the daily cruelty of the larger society in their social interactions with classmates. Voors believes the media are much to blame for the culture of cruelty. He explains, "The radio and TV airwaves are littered with trashtalking shock personalities who get their laughs from other people's miseries or disabilities."[96]

Voors explains that school climates of cruelty are enabled by adults, the media, and students who do not question society's standards. Enabling occurs in three ways. The first, he says, is normalization. That means believing that actions, attitudes, and offensive words are "normal" and acceptable. For example, there are laws protecting people from discrimination, but many people have prejudiced beliefs—and act on them—because they have never questioned the attitudes they were taught in society. They believe that their prejudices are normal and not even prejudices. The second enabler is minimization. It means making light of, or minimizing, insensitive or cruel behaviors and words. Voors says minimization includes such responses as "It's no big deal," or "Come on, I was just joking," or "It's just a part of school life." The last enabler is denial. Voors says denial can be a refusal to recognize one's prejudices and cruel behavior. Individuals have "blind spots" because they are too ashamed to face the truth of their own intolerance. People may also have blind spots about their school environment. Both adults and students may insist, "That kind of thing never happens here." Voors concludes that school social cruelty cannot be stopped until people learn to "name it," "confront it," and "realize that it is a big deal."[97]

Are High Schools to Blame?

Some social scientists blame the cruelty of school cliques not on larger society but on the way society organizes schools. Most experts want to improve schools, but Leon Botstein, the president of Bard College in New York, is an outspoken critic of high schools altogether. His conclusions are controversial with educators, but he says society should just get rid of high schools.

Botstein argues that students are forced into a "sports-dominated, clique-driven atmosphere" in which many are "outsiders, ostracized, and taunted by others." He adds, "By and large, the system gets an F. There are exceptions, but high school in general is a catastrophe, and we should abolish it as we know it." He insists that high schools cannot be fixed or made better. They teach young people to value the wrong things and do not prepare teens for the real world. Instead of helping teens to act maturely, schools treat teens like little babies. Botstein calls it "infantilizing"[98] them.

A GREAT MIX IT UP AT LUNCH DAY

"Black, white, Arab, non-Arab, bilingual, special education, jocks, musicians, it didn't matter. What did [matter] at that time was a group of human beings enjoying lunch, and taking a leap of faith in communication and bonding. One huge score for humanity." —Norma Harb, a social worker in Dearborn, Michigan.

Quoted in Teaching Tolerance, "Mix It Up: Score One for Humanity," Teaching Tolerance. www.tolerance.org/blog/mix-it-score-one-humanity.

Botstein calls for completely reinventing grades six through ten. He would eliminate middle school and end high school for students at age sixteen. Before that time, schools would just be elementary schools through grade six and then high school, starting with grade seven. Students would be grouped into very small classes that concentrated on discussion and analysis rather

Bard College president Leon Botstein has called for a complete reinvention of grades six through ten.

than grades and judgments of worth. From there, students could go directly to college.

With this kind of education, teens would stop concentrating on childish standards of popularity and appearance. Instead, they would value what matters in the real world, according to Botstein. He explains,

> High school is age-segregated. You coop up 18-year-olds and 17-year-olds by grade and you create a world where status is very important. "Oh, I'm a senior, you're just a junior." That's ludicrous. High school is an artificial world, a world of puerile [childish] notions of beauty and what is masculine or feminine. But universities and businesses are often led by people who were the outsiders in that world. Who's running Microsoft? The popular jocks? No. Probably the nerds. People in college begin to take their lives seriously. If they are interested in business, they start to admire [Microsoft founder] Bill Gates, or if it's science, then they admire [genetic scientists James] Watson and [Francis] Crick . They join the real conversation of life."[99]

Botstein believes that most teens are so segregated and isolated from real society in middle school and high school that they are forced to turn to cliques for self-protection. Then they obsess over who is popular, cool, or beautiful instead of concentrating on what matters. The cliques and peer pressure make it more difficult for teens to grow up.

Botstein calls middle school "idiotic" and high school a place that "demeans our young . . . and traps them in the vacuous [empty] world of teen culture." He says that schools today have failed to provide kind, interesting, and nurturing environments, and that is why students are so often unhappy. He says, "We don't teach them that the rules of real life are not the rules of Hollywood, not the rules of pop culture, and not the rules of high school."[100]

Outside the Box

Perhaps school cultures are ultimately responsible for the prevalence of exclusive cliques, but it is unlikely that high schools

Friendship groups are preferable to cliques because they value individuality and inclusivity.

and middle schools will be abolished anytime soon. What can students do to escape the artificial boxes that are created by the "rules" of school culture? Education specialist Marie Hartwell-Walker suggests that every teen search for a friendship group that is right for him or her rather than opt for an exclusive clique. The difference, she explains, is that friendship groups value differences and individuality. They are inclusive and welcome new friends, and they are tolerant of one another and held together by common interests.

Cliques, on the other hand, demand conformity and do not seek out new members. They use meanness to prove they are exclusive and superior. Sam, a young teen who was ostracized by her former clique, figured out the difference the hard way. She says, "I finally figured out that I have a right to be myself, not just what the group wants me to be."[101]

Teens can make individual decisions to be inclusive and to follow their own beliefs. According to a Pew Research poll conducted in 2007, young people today are already more tolerant and inclusive in their attitudes than those of any previous generation. The majority are accepting of immigrants, racial differences, and homosexuality.

If society is to blame for the climate of cruelty created by cliques, then perhaps it will be young people who change society. Teens can make decisions to be accepting of any differences, whether they are about looks, weight, skills, popularity, or social class. Perhaps the beginning of the end for the biases that cause clique cruelty lies with the youth of today.

Introduction: "Lunch Tray Moments"

1. Rosalind Wiseman, *Queen Bees & Wannabes*. New York: Crown, 2002, p. 9.
2. Wiseman, *Queen Bees & Wannabes*, p. 9.
3. Wiseman, *Queen Bees & Wannabes*, p. 21.

Chapter 1: Circle of Friends

4. Philip Guo, "On Popularity," Stanford University. www.stanford.edu/~pgbovine/popularity.htm.
5. Michael G. Thompson, "Peer Pleasure, Peer Pain," National Association of Independent Schools, Fall 1997, www.nais.org/publications/ismagazinearticle.cfm?ItemNumber=144253.
6. Joshua Mandel, "Social Life in Middle and High School: Dealing with Cliques and Bullies," Education.com, www.education.com/reference/article/bullying-in-middle-and-high-school.
7. Wiseman, *Queen Bees & Wannabes*, p. 19.
8. Charlene C. Giannetti and Margaret Sagarese, *Cliques*. New York: Broadway Books, 2001, p. 109.
9. Quoted in Wiseman, *Queen Bees & Wannabes*, p. 37.
10. Wiseman, *Queen Bees & Wannabes*, pp. 24, 33.
11. Michael Thompson and Lawrence J. Cohen, with Catherine O'Neill Grace, *Mom, They're Teasing Me*. New York: Ballantine, 2002, p. 171.
12. Giannetti and Sagarese, *Cliques*, p. 21.
13. Wiseman, *Queen Bees & Wannabes*, p. 30.
14. Quoted in "Margaret Sagarese on Cliques," AccessMyLibrary, November 1, 2001. www.accessmylibrary.com/article-1G1-113938028/margaret-sagarese-cliques-interview.html.
15. Quoted in Wiseman, *Queen Bees & Wannabes*, p. 183.
16. Greg Thomas, "Silly Rabbit, Cliques Are for Kids!" Open Sa-

lon, February 17, 2009. http://open.salon.com/blog/greg_thomas/2009/02/17/silly_rabbit_cliques_are_for_kids.

17. Quoted in Wiseman, *Queen Bees & Wannabes*, pp. 22–23.

18. Giannetti and Sagarese, *Cliques*, p. 8.

Chapter 2: Cliques and Social Cruelty

19. Carl E. Pickhardt, *The Everything Parent's Guide to Children and Divorce*. Avon, MA: Adams Media, F+W Publications, 2006, p. 200.

20. Quoted in Contactmusic.com, "Hayden Panettiere—Panettiere 'Tortured' by Jealous Schoolmates," Contactmusic.com, July 9, 2009. www.contactmusic.com/news.nsf/story/panettiere-tortured-by-jealous-schoolmates_1109279.

21. Quoted in Lynn Barker, "On the Set: Hayden Panettiere," SheKnows. www.sheknows.com/articles/809503.htm.

22. Quoted in Marsha Ginsburg, "Bay Area Teens Tell How Cruel School Life Can Be," *San Francisco Chronicle*, April 26, 1999. www.sfgate.com/cgi-bin/article/article?f=/e/a/1999/04/26/NEWS15935.dtl.

23. Robert Ruane, "If Your Kid Is Being Tormented at School—Read This," Epinions.com, May 3, 2005. www.epinions.com/kifm-review-7384-12659CF0-39C7D2E7-prod4.

24. Lawrence Cohen, "Hunters and Gatherers in the Classroom," National Association of Independent Schools, Fall 1997. www.nais.org/publications/ismagazinearticle.cfm?ItemNumber =144321.

25. Dana Williams, "Take the Sting out of Social Cruelty," *Teaching Tolerance*, 2002, www.sd151.k12.id.us/schools/oesweb/Anti-Bullying%20article.doc.

26. Ruane, "If Your Kid Is Being Tormented at School—Read This."

27. Jean Lawrence, "Girls Just Wanna Be Mean," MedicineNet.com, August 26, 2002. www.medicinenet.com/script/main/art.asp?articlekey=51829.

28. Giannetti and Sagarese, *Cliques*, p. 68.

29. Giannetti and Sagarese, *Cliques*, pp. 68, 70.

30. Victoria A. Brownworth, "Mean Girls Never Grow Up," *Curve*, April 2008. www.curvemag.com/Curve-Magazine/

April-2008/Mean-Girls-Never-Grow-Up.

31. Quoted in Melissa Beattie-Moss, "Fighting Back: Bullying Is Epidemic in American Schools—but It Can Be Prevented," ResearchPennState. www.rps.psu.edu/bullies/index.html.

32. Giannetti and Sagarese, *Cliques*, p. 7.

33. Giannetti and Sagarese, *Cliques*, pp. 125–26.

34. Wiseman, *Queen Bees & Wannabes*, p. 115.

35. Quoted in Sara Shandler, *Ophelia Speaks*. New York: Harper-Perennial, 1999, p. 155.

36. Thompson and Cohen, *Mom, They're Teasing Me*, pp. 62–63.

37. Wiseman, *Queen Bees & Wannabes*, p. 27.

38. Quoted in Wiseman, *Queen Bees & Wannabes*, pp. 293–94.

Chapter 3: Cliques and School Violence

39. Quoted in Caroline Alphonso, "Bullies Push Their Victims to Suicide," *Globe and Toronto Mail*, November 27, 2000. www .yorku.ca/lamarsh/news/02.htm.

40. Quoted in Teresa Mitchell, "Only Two Friends Said No," BNET, August–September 2002. http://findarticles.com/p/ articles/mi_m0OJX/is_1_27/ai_n25039269/?tag=content;col1.

41. Cindy Wesley, interview by Anderson Cooper, *The Point with Anderson Cooper*, CNN, March 28, 2002. http://transcripts .cnn.com/TRANSCRIPTS/0203/28/tpt.00.html.

42. John Halligan, "If We Only Knew, If Only He Told Us," Ryan's Story. www.ryanpatrickhalligan.org.

43. Quoted in Oprah.com, "When Sexual Bullying Turns Deadly," CNN.com, May 26, 2009. www.cnn.com/2009/ LIVING/personal/05/26/o.truth.about.bullying/index.html.

44. Wiseman, *Queen Bees & Wannabes*, p. 189.

45. Quoted in Rich Phillips, "Teen Says He's Sorry About Florida Boy's Burning," CNN, November 24, 2009. www.cnn.com/ 2009/CRIME/11/24/florida.burned.boy/index.html?eref=igo ogle_cnn.

46. San Diego County Office of Education, "Statistics & Facts: Did You Know?" www.sdcoe.net/vpi/stat.asp.

47. Quoted in Greg Toppo, "10 Years Later, The Real Story Be-

hind Columbine," *USA Today*, April 14, 2009. www.usatoday .com/news/nation/2009-04-13-columbine-myths_N.htm.

48. Beattie-Moss, "Fighting Back: Bullying Is Epidemic in American Schools—but It Can Be Prevented."

49. Quoted in Beattie-Moss, "Fighting Back: Bullying Is Epidemic in American Schools—but It Can Be Prevented."

50. Quoted in House Committee on the Judiciary, *Youth Culture and Violence*, 106th Cong., 1st sess., May 13, 1999. http:// commdocs.house.gov/committees/judiciary/hju62441.000/ hju62441_0f.htm.

51. Quoted in Terry McCarthy, "WARNING: Andy Williams Here. Unhappy Kid. Tired of Being Picked On," *Time*, March 11, 2001. www.time.com/time/magazine/article/0,9171,10 2077-1,00.html.

52. Quoted in Mark Zdechlik, "Friends of Alleged Shooter Think Teasing Was Final Straw," Minnesota Public Radio, September 25, 2003. http://news.minnesota.publicradio .org/features/2003/09/25_zdechlikm_reax.

53. Thompson and Cohen, *Mom, They're Teasing Me*, pp. 158–59.

54. Katherine Newman, interview by Amy Goodman, *Democracy Now!* May 8, 2007. www.democracynow.org/2007/ 5/8/katherine_newman_on_rampage_the_social.

55. Quoted in MentalHealthCES.com, "School Shootings: Ethical & Confidentiality Boundary Issues." http://homestudy credit.com/courses/contentSSE/trk SSE10.html.

56. Newman, interview by Amy Goodman.

57. Quoted in Mary-Lea Cox, "The Deadly Rampages of April," SSRC (Social Science Research Council), April 22, 2007.www.ssrc.org/features/view/the-deadly-rampages-of-april.

58. Quoted in Carly Rothman, "10 Years After Columbine School Shooting, N.J. Districts More Secure," Newark (NJ) *Star-Ledger*, April 20, 2009. www.nj.com/news/index.ssf/ 2009/04/10_years_after_columbine_schoo.html.

59. Quoted in Toppo, "10 Years Later, the Real Story Behind Columbine."

60. Wiseman, *Queen Bees & Wannabes*, p. 196.

61. Thompson and Cohen, *Mom, They're Teasing Me*, p. 160.

Chapter 4: Can Cliques Be Discouraged?

62. Jane Bluestein, "Pretty and Popular," JaneBluestein.com. www.janebluestein.com/articles/popular.html.
63. Quoted in Bluestein, "Pretty and Popular."
64. Kalli Gibbs, "Jackson High School Senior Believes School Uniforms Should Be a Mandatory Requirement," *Southeast Missourian*, January 9, 2007. www.semissourian.com/story/1184433.html.
65. Marian Wilde, "Do Uniforms Make Schools Better?" Great Schools. www.greatschools.org/find-a-school/defining-your-ideal/school-uniforms.gs?content=121&page=1.
66. Quoted in Joseph DiSalvo, "School Uniforms: Still a Good Idea," San Jose Inside, September 8, 2009. www.sanjoseinside.com/sji/blog/entries/school_uniforms_still_a_good_idea.
67. Julia Wilkins, "School Uniforms—Not Clear That School Uniforms Will Reduce Violence," BNET, March 1999. http://findarticles.com/p/articles/mi_m1374/is_2_59/ai_54099133/pg_5/?tag=content;col1.
68. Julia Wilkins, "School Uniforms—Not Clear That School Uniforms Will Reduce Violence."
69. David J. Jamison, "Idols of the Tribe: Brand Veneration, Group Identity, and the Impact of School Uniform Policies," *Academy of Marketing Studies Journal*, vol. 10, no. 1, 2006. www.alliedacademies.org/Publications/Papers/AMSJ%20Vol%2010%20 No%201%202006%20p%2019-41.pdf.
70. Jamison, "Idols of the Tribe."
71. Eddie Baumann and Abby Baumann, "Middle Schoolers and Cliques: The Good, the Bad, and Avoiding the Ugly," CSE Convention Special, Cedarville University, 2005–2006. http://ctl.cedarville.edu/tep/baumann/files/edu6000/article_MiddleSchoolCliques.pdf.
72. Giannetti and Sagarese, *Cliques*, pp. 215–16.
73. Giannetti and Sagarese, *Cliques*, p. 216.
74. Quoted in Giannetti and Sagarese, *Cliques*, p. 221.
75. Giannetti and Sagarese, *Cliques*, p. 120.
76. Giannetti and Sagarese, *Cliques*, pp. 137–40.

77. Quoted in Sharon Cromwell, "Mix It Up at Lunch Day Teaches Tolerance," Education World, April 20, 2009. www.educationworld.com/a_admin/admin/admin563.shtml.

78. Teaching Tolerance, "Mix It Up." www.tolerance.org/mix-it-up.

79. Teaching Tolerance, "Mix It Up."

80. Quoted in Cromwell, "Mix It Up at Lunch Day Teaches Tolerance."

Chapter 5: Society and the Development of Cliques

81. Wilkins, "School Uniforms."

82. Luke Jackson, *Freaks, Geeks & Asperger Syndrome*. London: Kingsley, 2002, p. 149.

83. Jackson, *Freaks, Geeks & Asperger Syndrome*, pp. 135–36.

84. Quoted in James Crisp, "Fairytale Ending for Girl Who Defied Yobs," *Macclesfield Express*, August 2, 2006. www.macclesfield-express.co.uk/news/s/515/515914_fairytale_ending_for_girl_who_defied_yobs.html.

85. Quoted in Anushka Asthana, "Crackdown on Schoolgirl Bullying Epidemic," *Observer* (London), January 20, 2008. www.guardian.co.uk/uk/2008/jan/20/pupilbehaviour.gender.

86. Phil Beadle, "Battle to Beat the Last Acceptable Prejudice," *Guardian* (Manchester, UK) January 20, 2009. www.guardian.co.uk/education/2009/jan/20/homophobia-schools-british-beadle-phil.

87. Philipp Aschauer, "The Myth of High School Cliques," Philafication, June 1, 2008. http://philafication.com/.

88. Aschauer, "The Myth of High School Cliques."

89. Timothy P. Daniels, *Building Cultural Nationalism in Malaysia: Identity, Representation, and Citizenship*. New York: Routledge, 2005, p. 216.

90. Quoted in Bluestein, "Pretty and Popular."

91. Bluestein, "Pretty and Popular."

92. Quoted in Bluestein, "Pretty and Popular."

93. Quoted in Kate Bedford, "Jane Bluestein Discusses Emotionally Safe Schools," JaneBluestein.com, 2001. www.janebluestein.com/articles/interview.html.

94. Thompson and Cohen, *Mom, They're Teasing Me*, p. 191.

95. Giannetti and Sagarese, *Cliques*, pp. 146–47.
96. William Voors, "Confronting Cultures of Cruelty," *Paradigm*, Winter 2004. www.narsadartworks.org/article.pdf.
97. Voors, "Confronting Cultures of Cruelty."
98. Quoted in Patrick Rogers, "Enough Already," *People*, July 12, 1999. www.people.com/people/archive/article/0,,2012 8698,00.html.
99. Quoted in Rogers, "Enough Already."
100. Quoted in Robert Epstein, "Why High Schools Must Go: An Interview with Leon Botstein," *Phi Delta Kappan*, May 2007. www.iperbole.bologna.it/iperbole/adi/XoopsAdi/up loads/PDdownloads/interview_with_botstein.pdf.
101. Quoted in Marie Hartwell-Walker, "Click or Clique: Positive and Negative Teen Social Groups," PsychCentral. http://psychcentral.com/lib/2008/click-or-clique-positive-and-negative-teen-social-groups/all/1.

DISCUSSION QUESTIONS

Chapter 1: Circle of Friends

1. Are there exclusive cliques in your school? Why or why not?
2. Is your circle of friends a group or a clique?
3. What are some advantages and disadvantages of clique membership?

Chapter 2: Cliques and Social Cruelty

1. Can you give any examples of social cruelty, either from your own experiences or from incidents that happened to someone else?
2. Is popularity always related to social cruelty or relational aggression? Why or why not?
3. How do bystanders contribute to social cruelty and relational aggression?

Chapter 3: Cliques and School Violence

1. At what point does clique aggression and bullying deserve to be called a crime?
2. What is the difference between a lone bully and a bullying clique (besides the obvious one of number)?
3. Do you believe that school shootings are caused by mean cliques? Why or why not?

Chapter 4: Can Cliques Be Discouraged?

1. Would you resent or approve of a mandatory dress code or school uniform policy? Why?
2. What acts of kindness can bystanders choose in order to minimize or stop clique cruelty?
3. Could there be inclusive cliques? How would they work?

Chapter 5: Society and the Development of Cliques

1. How are cliques in other countries different from U.S. cliques? How are they the same?
2. How are these concepts related: prejudice, intolerance, discrimination, disrespect, and exclusiveness?
3. What does the society of your school do to fight exclusiveness and social cruelty? What would you like to see change?

ORGANIZATIONS TO CONTACT

Boys Town National Hotline
14100 Crawford Street
Boys Town, Nebraska 68010
Phone: 800-448-3000
Web site: www.boystown.org

Anyone, boy or girl, can call the Boys Town National Hotline at any time to get help and support for any problem. People who are feeling depressed, isolated, or suicidal can talk to trained counselors and figure out what to do.

Gay, Lesbian and Straight Education Network (GLSEN)
122 West 26th Street, Suite 1100
New York, New York 10001
Phone: 212-727-0135
Web site: www.glsen.org

GLSEN works to promote safe schools in which each student is valued and respected. It provides extensive antibullying advice and runs the campaign "Think Before You Speak."

i-SAFE Inc.
5900 Pasteur Court, Suite #100
Carlsbad, California 92008
Phone: 760-603-7911
Web site: www.isafe.org

I-SAFE promotes Internet safety and provides information about how to avoid inappropriate, harassing, or criminal behavior online.

Olweus Bullying Prevention Program
Clemson University
Clemson, South Carolina 29634
Phone: 800-328-9000
Web site: www.olweus.org

The Olweus Bullying Prevention Program is designed to help schools reduce bullying and improve the social climate in schools. Its Web site provides much information about bullying and the goals of the program.

Teaching Tolerance
400 Washington Avenue
Montgomery, Alabama 36104
Phone: 334-956-8200
Web site:www.tolerance.org

Teaching Tolerance provides free educational materials to fight prejudice and encourage equality. It also sponsors the national Mix It Up program for schools.

Books

David Borgenicht, Robin Epstein, and Ben H. Winters, *Worst-Case Scenario Survival Guide.* San Francisco, CA: Chronicle, 2009. With humor and cartoons, the authors of this book detail everything you need to know about middle school, including bullies and cliques.

Sharon Gunton, ed., *Social Issues Firsthand: Cliques.* Farmington Hills, MI: Greenhaven Press, 2009. With personal stories and professional advice, this book explores cliques from different individual perspectives.

Jill Hamilton, ed., *Issues That Concern You: Bullying and Hazing.* Farmington Hills, MI: Greenhaven Press, 2008. Different experts discuss the issues of social cruelty and violence. Hazing (initiations that can become dangerous and violent) and bullying are explored from different points of view, such as whether they can be stopped and what are the root causes of the behavior.

Erika V. Shearin Karres, *Mean Chicks, Cliques, and Dirty Tricks: A Real Girl's Guide to Getting Through It All.* 2nd ed. Avon, MA: Adams Media, 2010. This book is a "survival guide" for girls, discussing cliques, teasing, peer pressure, bullying, and much more. With humor, quizzes, and practical advice, the author attempts to empower girls as they cope with school social life.

Norah Piehl, ed., *Social Issues Firsthand: Bullying.* Farmington Hills, MI: Greenhaven Press, 2009. This book is a compilation of articles about the issue of bullying and violence among young people.

Rachel Simmons, *Odd Girl Speaks Out: Girls Write About Bullies, Cliques, Popularity, and Jealousy.* Orlando, FL: Harcourt, 2004. The author has collected the stories, anecdotes, poems, and letters of teen girls describing the aggression and meanness that girls inflict on other girls. Experiences are related from different points of view.

Internet Sources

Smartgirl, "Report on Cliques and Friend Groups: Your Experiences." www.smartgirl.org/reports/7685873.html.

Student News A to Z with Carl Azuz, "Uncliquing Cliques," CNN Student News. http://cnnstudentnews.blogs.cnn.com/2007/11/14/uncliquing-cliques/.

TeensHealth, "Coping with Cliques." http://kidshealth.org/teen/your_mind/problems/cliques.html#.

Web Sites

girlshealth.gov (www.girlshealth.gov). Visitors to this large site can explore girls' issues, including dealing with relationships and bullying.

The Ophelia Project (www.opheliaproject.org). The Ophelia Project is dedicated to fighting relational aggression in schools, at home, and in society.

Stop Bullying Now! (www.stopbullyingnow.hrsa.gov). This government Web site discusses all kinds of bullying—what it is, why people do it, and how to stop it. There are separate sections for kids and adults.

Teaching Tolerance: Test Yourself for Hidden Bias (http://www.tolerance.org/activity/test-yourself-hidden-bias). Starting at this page, visitors can access Project Implicit's Web site and take a variety of anonymous tests to explore their hidden biases. The tests take some time but may reveal interesting, unconscious biases.

INDEX

PICTURE CREDITS

ABOUT THE AUTHOR

Toney Allman holds a bachelor of science degree in psychology from Ohio State University and master of arts degree in clinical psychology from the University of Hawaii. She currently lives in Virginia and writes books for students on a variety of topics.